PRAISE FOR CRUCIAL CONVERSATIONS

"Relationships are the priority of life, and conversations are the crucial element in profound caring of relationships. This book helps us to think about what we really want to say. If you want to succeed in both talking and listening, read this book."

—Dr. Lloyd J. Ogilvie, chaplain, United States Senate

"Important, lucid, and practical, *Crucial Conversations* is a book that will make a difference in your life. Learn how to flourish in every difficult situation."

—Robert E. Quinn, ME Tracy Collegiate Professor of OBHRM, University of Michigan Business School

"I was personally and professionally inspired by this book—and I'm not easily impressed. In the fast-paced world of IT, the success of our systems, and our business, depends on crucial conversations we have every day. Unfortunately, because our environment is so technical, far too often we forget about the 'human systems' that make or break us. These skills are the missing foundation piece."

—Maureen Burke, manager of training, Coca-Cola Enterprises, Inc.

"The book is compelling. Yes, I found myself in too many of their examples of what not to do when caught in these worst-of-all-worlds situations! GET THIS BOOK, WHIP OUT A PEN AND GET READY TO SCRIBBLE MARGIN NOTES FURIOUSLY, AND PRACTICE, PRACTICE, PRACTICE THE INVALUABLE TOOLS THESE AUTHORS PRESENT. I know I did—and it helped me salvage several difficult situations and repair my damaged self-esteem in others. I will need another copy pretty soon, as I'm wearing out the pages in this one!"

—James Belasco, best-selling author of *Flight of the Buffalo*, entrepreneur, professor, and executive director of the Financial Times Knowledge Dialogue

Crucial
Conversations

Crucial Conversations

Tools for Talking
When Stakes Are High

by

Kerry Patterson, Joseph Grenny,
Ron McMillan, and Al Switzler

McGraw-Hill

New York   Chicago   San Francisco   Lisbon
London   Madrid   Mexico City   Milan   New Delhi
San Juan   Seoul   Singapore   Sydney   Toronto

Library of Congress Cataloging-in-Publication Data

Crucial Conversations : tools for talking when stakes are high / Kerry
Patterson ... [et al.].
    p.   cm.
    Includes bibliographical references and index.
    ISBN 0-07-140194-6
    1. International communication.   2. Interpersonal relations.   I.
Patterson, Kerry, 1946-

    BF637.C45.C78   2002
    153.6—dc21   2002001129

McGraw-Hill

A Division of The McGraw·Hill Companies

31 32 33 34 35   DOC/DOC   0 9 8 7

ISBN 0-07-140194-6

*This book was set in R Life Roman by Patricia Caruso of McGraw-Hill Professional's
DTP composition unit in Hightstown, N.J.*

Printed and bound by R.R. Donnelly & Sons Company.

McGraw-Hill books are available at special quantity discounts to use as premiums and
sales promotions, or for use in corporate training programs. For more information,
please write to the Director of Special Sales, Professional Publishing, McGraw-Hill,
Two Penn Plaza, New York, NY 10121-2298. Or contact your local bookstore.

We dedicate this book to
Louise, Celia, Bonnie, and Linda—

whose support is abundant,
whose love is nourishing,
and whose patience is just shy of infinite.

And to our children

Christine, Rebecca, Taylor, Scott,
Aislinn, Cara, Seth, Samuel, Hyrum,
Amber, Megan, Chase, Hayley, Bryn,
Amber, Laura, Becca, Rachael, Benjamin,
Meridith, Lindsey, Kelley, Todd
who have been a wonderful source of learning.

Contents

Foreword

This is a breakthrough book. That is exactly how I saw it when I first read the manuscript. I so resonated with the importance, power, and timeliness of its message that I even suggested to the authors that they title it "Breakthrough Conversations." But as I read deeper, listened to the tapes, and experienced the insight borne of years of experience with this material, I came to understand why it is titled *Crucial Conversations*.

From my own work with organizations, including families, and from my own experience, I have come to see that there are a few defining moments in our lives and careers that make all the difference. Many of these defining moments come from "crucial" or "breakthrough" conversations with important people in emotionally charged situations where the decisions made take us down one of several roads, each of which leads to an entirely different destination.

I can see the wisdom in the assertion of the great historian Arnold Toynbee, who said that you can pretty well summarize all of history—not only of society, but of institutions and of people—in four words: *Nothing fails like success*. In other words, when a challenge in life is met by a response that is equal to it, you have success. But when the challenge moves to a higher level, the old, once successful response no longer works—it fails; thus, nothing fails like success.

The challenge has noticeably changed for our lives, our families, and our organizations. Just as the world is changing at frightening speed and has become increasingly and profoundly interdependent with marvelous and dangerous technologies, so, too, have the stresses and pressures we all experience exponentially increased. This charged atmosphere makes it all the more imperative that we nourish our relationships and develop tools, skills, and enhanced capacity to find *new* and better solutions to our problems.

These newer, better solutions will not represent "my way" or "your way"—they will represent "our way." In short, the solutions must be synergistic, meaning that the whole is greater than the sum of the parts. Such synergy may manifest itself in a better decision, a better relationship, a better decision-making process, increased commitment to implement decisions made, or a combination of two or more of these.

What you learn is that "crucial conversations" *transform* people and relationships. They are anything but *transacted*; they create an entirely new level of bonding. They produce what Buddhism calls "the middle way"—not a compromise between two opposites on a straight-line continuum, but a higher middle way, like the apex of a triangle. Because two or more people have created something new from genuine dialogue, bonding takes place—just like the bonding that takes place in family or marriage when a new child is created. When you produce something with another person that is truly creative, it's one of the most powerful forms of bonding there is. In fact the bonding is so strong that you simply would not be disloyal in his or her *absence*, even if there were social pressure to join others in badmouthing.

The sequential development of the subject matter in this book is brilliant. It moves you from understanding the supernal power of dialogue, to clarifying what you really want to have happen and focusing on what actually is happening, to creating conditions of safety, to using self-awareness and self-knowledge. And finally, it moves you to learning how to achieve such a level of mutual understanding and creative synergy that people are emotionally connected to the conclusions reached and are emotionally willing and committed to effectively implementing them. In short, you move from creating the right mind- and heart-set to developing and utilizing the right skill-set.

In spite of the fact that I have spent many years writing and teaching similar ideas, I found myself being deeply influenced, motivated, and even inspired by this material—learning new ideas, going deeper into old ideas, seeing new applications, and broadening my understanding. I've also learned how these new techniques, skills, and tools work together in enabling crucial conversations that truly create a break with the mediocrity or mistakes of the past. Most *breakthroughs* in life truly are "break-withs."

When I first put my hands on this book, I was delighted to see that dear friends and colleagues had drawn on their entire lives and professional experiences to not only address a tremendously important topic, but also to do it in a way that is so accessible, so fun, so full of humor and illustration, so full of common sense and practicality. They show how to effectively blend and use both intellectual (I.Q.) and emotional intelligence (E.Q.) to enable crucial conversations.

I remember one of the authors having a crucial conversation with his professor in college. The professor felt that this student was neither paying the price in class nor living up to his potential. This student, my friend, listened carefully, restated the professor's concern, expressed appreciation for the professor's affirmation of his potential, and then smilingly and calmly said, "My focus is on other priorities, and the class is just not that important to me at this time. I hope you can understand." The teacher was taken aback, but then started to listen. A dialogue took place, new understanding was achieved, and the bonding was deepened.

I know these authors to be outstanding individuals and remarkable teachers and consultants, and have even seen them work their magic in training seminars—but I didn't know if they could take this complex topic and fit it into a book. They did. I encourage you to really dig into this material, to pause and think deeply about each part and how the parts are sequenced. Then apply what you've learned, go back to the book again, learn some more, and apply your new learnings. Remember, to *know* and not to *do* is really not to know.

I think you'll discover, as have I, that crucial conversations, as powerfully described in this book, reflect the insight of this excerpt of Robert Frost's beautiful and memorable poem, "The Road Not Taken":

> *Two roads diverged in a yellow wood,*
> *And sorry I could not travel both*
> *And be one traveler, long I stood*
> *And looked down one as far as I could*
> *To where it bent in the undergrowth; . . .*
>
> *I shall be telling this with a sigh*
> *Somewhere ages and ages hence:*
> *Two roads diverged in a wood, and I—*
> *I took the one less traveled by,*
> *And that has made all the difference.*

— Stephen R. Covey

Acknowledgments

We are deeply grateful to many.

First, to our colleagues at VitalSmarts, we express appreciation for creativity, discipline, competence, and friendship. Thanks to Charla Allen, James Allred, Mike Carter, Benson Dastrup, Kevin Koger, Kevin Sheehan, Jed Thompson, Mindy Waite, and Yan Wang.

Also we appreciate our colleagues for their indispensable help in teaching and testing these ideas: Bernell Christensen, Larry Myler, Bev Roesch, and Steve Willis.

And to our associate friends who have worked hard to change lives and organizations with these concepts—and provided invaluable feedback for refining them: Mike Allen, Karol Bailey, Pat Banks, Mike Cook, Brint Driggs, Simon Lia, Mike Miller, Jim Munoa, Stacy Nelson, Larry Peters, Betsy Pickren, Mike Quinlan, Ron Ragain, James Sanwick, Kurt Southam, Neil Staker, Joe Thigpen, and Michael Thompson.

Thanks to our agent, Michael Broussard, for getting us the opportunity to share our message. And thanks to our editor, Nancy Hancock, a world-class partner in producing this book and a master of crucial conversations.

And one final, sweeping, large thanks. So many have helped us over the years, that we add this admittedly blanket thanks to the clients, colleagues, friends, teachers, and associates on whose shoulders we stand.

1

> *The void created by the failure to communicate is soon filled with poison, drivel, and misrepresentation.*
>
> —C. NORTHCOTE PARKINSON

What's a Crucial Conversation?

And Who Cares?

When people first hear the term "crucial conversation," many conjure up images of presidents, emperors, and prime ministers seated around a massive table while they debate the future of the world. Although it's true that such discussions have a wide-sweeping and lasting impact, they're not the kind we have in mind. The crucial conversations we're referring to in the title of this book are interactions that happen to everyone. They're the day-to-day conversations that affect your life.

Now, what makes one of your conversations crucial as opposed to plain vanilla? First, *opinions vary*. For example, you're talking with your boss about a possible promotion. She thinks you're not ready; you think you are. Second, *stakes are high*. You're in a meeting with four coworkers and you're trying to pick a new marketing strategy. You've got to do something different or your company isn't going to hit its annual goals. Third, *emotions run strong*. You're in the middle of a casual discussion with your spouse and he or she brings up an "ugly incident" that took place at yesterday's neighborhood block party. Apparently not only did you flirt with someone at the party, but according to your spouse, "You were practically making out." You don't remember flirting. You simply remember being polite and friendly. Your spouse walks off in a huff.

And speaking of the block party, at one point you're making small talk with your somewhat crotchety and always colorful neighbor about his shrinking kidneys when he says, "Speaking of the new fence you're building . . ." From that moment on you end up in a heated debate over placing the new fence—three inches one way or the other. Three inches! He finishes by threatening you with a lawsuit, and you punctuate your points by mentioning that he's not completely aware of the difference between his hind part and his elbow. Emotions run *really* strong.

What makes each of these conversations crucial—and not simply challenging, frustrating, frightening, or annoying—is that the results could have a huge impact on the quality of your life. In each case, some element of your daily routine could be forever altered for better or worse. Clearly a promotion could make a big difference. Your company's success affects you and everyone you work with. Your relationship with your spouse influences every aspect of your life. Even something as trivial as a debate over a property line affects how you get along with your neighbor. If you handle even a seemingly insignificant conversation poorly, you establish a pattern of behavior that shows up in all of your crucial conversations.

By definition, crucial conversations are about tough issues. Unfortunately, it's human nature to back away from discussions we fear will hurt us or make things worse. We're masters at avoiding these tough conversations. Coworkers send email to each other when they should walk down the hall and talk turkey. Bosses leave voice mail in lieu of meeting with their direct reports. Family members change the subject when an issue gets too risky. We (the authors) have a friend who learned through a voice-mail message that his wife was divorcing him. We use all kinds of tactics to dodge touchy issues.

But it doesn't have to be this way. If you know how to handle (even master) crucial conversations, you can step up to and effectively hold tough conversations about virtually any topic.

> **Crucial Conversation** (krōō shel kän'vŭr sā'shen) *n*
> A discussion between two or more people where (1) stakes are high, (2) opinions vary, and (3) emotions run strong.

HOW DO WE TYPICALLY HANDLE CRUCIAL CONVERSATIONS?

Just because we're in the middle of a crucial conversation (or maybe thinking about stepping up to one) doesn't mean that we're in trouble or that we won't fare well. In truth, when we face crucial conversations, we can do one of three things:

- We can avoid them.
- We can face them and handle them poorly.
- We can face them and handle them well.

That seems simple enough. Walk away from crucial conversations and suffer the consequences. Handle them poorly and suffer the consequences. Or handle them well.

"I don't know," you think to yourself. "Given the three choices, I'll go with handling them well."

We're on Our Worst Behavior

But do we handle them well? When talking turns tough, do we pause, take a deep breath, announce to our innerselves, "Uh-oh, this discussion is crucial. I'd better pay close attention" and then trot out our best behavior? Or when we're anticipating a potentially dangerous discussion, do we step up to it rather than scamper away? Sometimes. Sometimes we boldly step up to hot topics, monitor our behavior, and offer up our best work. We mind our Ps and Qs. Sometimes we're just flat-out *good*.

And then we have the rest of our lives. These are the moments when, for whatever reason, we either anticipate a crucial conversation or are in the middle of one and we're at our absolute worst—we yell; we withdraw; we say things we later regret. When conversations matter the most—that is, when conversations move from casual to crucial—we're generally on our worst behavior.

Why is that?

We're designed wrong. When conversations turn from routine to crucial, we're often in trouble. That's because emotions don't exactly prepare us to converse effectively. Countless generations of genetic shaping drive humans to handle crucial conversations with flying fists and fleet feet, not intelligent persuasion and gentle attentiveness.

For instance, consider a typical crucial conversation. Someone says something you disagree with about a topic that matters a great deal to you and the hairs on the back of your neck stand up. The *hairs* you can handle. Unfortunately, your body does more. Two tiny organs seated neatly atop your kidneys pump adrenaline into your bloodstream. You don't *choose* to do this. Your adrenal glands do it, and then you have to live with it.

And that's not all. Your brain then diverts blood from activities it deems nonessential to high-priority tasks such as hitting and running. Unfortunately, as the large muscles of the arms and legs get *more* blood, the higher-level reasoning sections of your brain get *less*. As a result, you end up facing challenging conversations with the same equipment available to a rhesus monkey.

We're under pressure. Let's add another factor. Crucial conversations are frequently spontaneous. More often than not, they come out of nowhere. And since you're caught by surprise, you're forced to conduct an extraordinarily complex human interaction in real time—no books, no coaches, and certainly no short breaks while a team of therapists runs to your aid and pumps you full of nifty ideas.

What *do* you have to work with? The issue at hand, the other person, and a brain that's preparing to fight or take flight. It's little wonder that we often say and do things that make perfect sense in the moment, but later on seem, well, stupid.

"What was I thinking?" you wonder.

The truth is, you were real-time multitasking with a brain that was working another job. You're lucky you didn't suffer a stroke.

We're stumped. Now let's throw in one more complication. You don't know where to start. You're making this up as you go along because you haven't often seen real-life models of effective communication skills. Let's say that you actually planned for a tough conversation—maybe you've even mentally rehearsed. You feel prepared, and you're as cool as a cucumber. Will you succeed? Not necessarily. You can still screw up, because practice doesn't make perfect; *perfect* practice makes perfect.

This means that first you have to know what to practice. Sometimes you don't. After all, you may have never actually seen how a certain problem is best handled. You may have seen what *not* to do—as modeled by a host of friends, colleagues, and, yes, even your parents. In fact, you may have sworn time and again not to act the same way.

Left with no healthy models, you're now more or less stumped. So what do you do? You do what most people do. You wing it. You piece together the words, create a certain mood, and otherwise make up what you think will work—all the while multiprocessing with a half-starved brain. It's little wonder that when it matters the most, we're often at our worst behavior.

We act in self-defeating ways. In our doped-up, dumbed-down state, the strategies we choose for dealing with our crucial conversations are perfectly designed to keep us from what we actually want. We're our own worst enemies—and we don't even realize it. Here's how this works.

Let's say that your significant other has been paying less and less attention to you. You realize he or she has a busy job, but you still would like more time together. You drop a few hints about the issue, but your loved one doesn't handle it well. You decide not to put on added pressure, so you clam up. Of course, since you're not all that happy with the arrangement, your displeasure now comes out through an occasional sarcastic remark.

"Another late night, huh? Do you really need all of the money in the world?"

Unfortunately (and here's where the problem becomes self-defeating), the more you snip and snap, the less your loved one wants to be around you. So your significant other spends even less time with you, you become even more upset, and the spiral continues. Your behavior is now actually creating the very thing you didn't want in the first place. You're caught in an unhealthy, self-defeating loop.

Or consider what's happening with your roommate Terry—who wears your and your other two roommates' clothes (without asking)—and he's proud of it. In fact, one day while walking out the door, he glibly announced that he was wearing something from each of your closets. You could see Taylor's pants, Scott's shirt, and, yes, even Chris's new matching shoes-and-socks ensemble. What of yours could he possibly be wearing? Eww!

Your response, quite naturally, has been to bad-mouth Terry behind his back. That is until one day when he overheard you belittling him to a friend, and you're now so embarrassed that you avoid being around him. Now when you're out of the apartment, he wears your clothes, eats your food, and uses your computer out of spite.

Let's try another example. You share a cubicle with a four-star slob and you're a bit of a neat freak. In *Odd Couple* parlance, you're Felix and he's Oscar. Your coworker has left you notes written in grease pencil on your file cabinet, in catsup on the back of a french-fry bag, and in permanent marker on your desk blotter. You, in contrast, leave him typed Post-it notes. Typed.

At first you sort of tolerated each other. Then you began to get on each other's nerves. You started nagging him about cleaning up. He started nagging you about your nagging. Now you're beginning to react to each other. Every time you nag, he becomes upset, and, well, let's say that he doesn't exactly clean up. Every time he calls you an "anal-retentive nanny," you vow not to give in to his vile and filthy ways.

What has come from all this bickering? Now you're neater than ever, and your cubicle partner's half of the work area is about to be condemned by the health department. You're caught in a self-defeating loop. The more the two of you push each other, the more you create the very behaviors you both despise.

Some Common Crucial Conversations

In each of these examples of unhealthy self-perpetuation, the stakes were moderate to high, opinions varied, and emotions ran strong. Actually, to be honest, in a couple of the examples the stakes were fairly low at first, but with time and growing emotions, the relationship eventually turned sour and quality of life suffered—making the risks high.

These examples, of course, are merely the tip of an enormous and ugly iceberg of problems stemming from crucial conversations that either have been avoided or have gone wrong. Other topics that could easily lead to disaster include

- Ending a relationship
- Talking to a coworker who behaves offensively or makes suggestive comments
- Asking a friend to repay a loan
- Giving the boss feedback about her behavior
- Approaching a boss who is breaking his own safety or quality policies
- Critiquing a colleague's work
- Asking a roommate to move out
- Resolving custody or visitation issues with an ex-spouse
- Dealing with a rebellious teen
- Talking to a team member who isn't keeping commitments
- Discussing problems with sexual intimacy
- Confronting a loved one about a substance abuse problem
- Talking to a colleague who is hoarding information or resources
- Giving an unfavorable performance review
- Asking in-laws to quit interfering
- Talking to a coworker about a personal hygiene problem

OUR AUDACIOUS CLAIM

Let's say that either you avoid tough issues or when you do bring them up, you're on your worst behavior. What's the big deal? How high are the stakes anyway? Do the consequences of a fouled-up conversation extend beyond the conversation itself? Should you worry?

Actually, the effects of conversations gone bad can be both devastating and far reaching. Our research has shown that strong relationships, careers, organizations, and communities all draw from the same source of power—the ability to talk openly about high-stakes, emotional, controversial topics.

So here's the audacious claim. Master your crucial conversations and you'll kick-start your career, strengthen your relationships, and improve your health. As you and others master high-stakes discussions, you'll also vitalize your organization and your community.

Kick-Start Your Career

Could the ability to master crucial conversations help your career? Absolutely. Twenty-five years of research with twenty thousand people and hundreds of organizations has taught us that individuals who are the most influential—who can get things done, *and at the same time* build on relationships—are those who master their crucial conversations.

For instance, high performers know how to stand up to the boss without committing career suicide. We've all seen people hurt their careers over tough issues. You may have done it yourself. Fed up with a lengthy and unhealthy pattern of behavior, you finally speak out—but a bit too abruptly. Oops. Or maybe an issue becomes so hot that as your peers twitch and fidget themselves into a quivering mass of potential stroke victims, you decide to say something. It's not a pretty discussion—but somebody has to have the guts to keep the boss from doing something stupid. (Gulp.)

As it turns out, you don't have to choose between being honest and being effective. You don't have to choose between candor and your career. People who routinely hold crucial conversations and hold them well are able to express controversial and even risky opinions in a way that gets heard. Their bosses, peers, and direct reports listen without becoming defensive or angry.

What about your career? Are there crucial conversations that you're not holding or not holding well? Is this undermining your influence? And more importantly, would your career take a step forward if you could improve how you're dealing with these conversations?

Improve Your Organization

Okay, so individual careers may sink or swim based on crucial conversations, but how about organizations? Surely a soft-and-gushy factor such as how you talk to one another doesn't have an impact on the not so soft-and-gushy bottom line.

For twenty-five years we (the authors) explored this very issue. We (and hundreds of others) searched for keys to organizational success. Most of us studying the elusive topic figured that something as large as a company's overall success would depend on something as large as a company's strategy, structure, or systems.

After all, organizations that maintain best-in-class productivity rely on elegant performance-management systems. Widespread productivity couldn't result from anything less, could it? We weren't alone in our thinking. Every organization that attempted to bring about improvements—at least the companies we had heard of—began by revamping their performance-management systems.

Then we actually studied those who had invested heavily in spiffy new performance-management systems. It turns out that we were dead wrong. Changing structures and systems alone did little to improve performance. For example, one study of five hundred stunningly productive organizations revealed that peak performance had absolutely nothing to do with forms, procedures, and policies that drive performance management. In fact, half of the highflyers had almost *no* formal performance-management processes.[1]

What's behind their success? It all comes down to how people handle crucial conversations. Within high-performing companies, when employees fail to deliver on their promises, colleagues willingly and effectively step in to discuss the problem. In the *worst* companies, poor performers are first ignored and then transferred. In *good* companies, bosses eventually deal with problems. In the *best* companies, everyone holds everyone else accountable—regardless of level or position. The path to high productivity passes not through a static system, but through face-to-face conversations at all levels.

Solve pressing problems. The best companies in almost any critical area are the ones that have developed the skills for dealing effectively with conversations that relate to that specific topic. For example:

- *Safety.* When someone violates a procedure or otherwise acts in an unsafe way, the first person to see the problem, regardless of his or her position, steps up and holds a crucial conversation.

- *Productivity.* If an employee underperforms, fails to live up to a promise, doesn't carry his or her fair share, or simply isn't productive enough, the affected parties address the problem immediately.

- *Diversity.* When someone feels offended, threatened, insulted, or harassed, he or she skillfully and comfortably, discusses the issue with the offending party.

- *Quality.* In companies where quality rules, people discuss problems face-to-face when they first come up.

- *Every other hot topic.* Companies that are best-in-class in innovation, teamwork, change management, or any other area that calls for human interaction are best-in-class in holding the relevant crucial conversations.

What's the relationship between success in a key area and crucial conversations? Companies that make impressive improvements in key performance areas (and eventually master them) are generally no different than others in their efforts to improve. They conduct the same awareness training, print the same banners, and make the same speeches. They differ in what happens when someone does something wrong. Rather than waiting for a policy to kick in or a leader to take charge, people step up, speak up, and thrive. Equally important, if it's a leader who seems to be out of line, employees willingly speak up, the problem is solved, and the company moves on.

So what about you? Is your organization stuck in its progress toward some important goal? If so, are there conversations that you're either avoiding or botching? And how about the people you work with? Are they stepping up to or walking away from crucial conversations? Could you take a big step forward by improving how you deal with these conversations?

Improve Your Relationships

Consider the impact crucial conversations can have on your relationships. Could failed crucial conversations lead to failed relationships? As it turns out, when you ask the average person what causes couples to break up, he or she usually suggests that it's due to differences of opinion. You know, people have different theories about how to manage their finances, spice up their love lives, or rear their children. In truth, *everyone* argues about important issues. But not everyone splits up. It's *how* you argue that matters.

For example, when Clifford Notarius and Howard Markman (two noted marriage scholars) examined couples in the throes of heated discussions, they learned that people fall into three categories—those who digress into threats and name-calling, those who revert to silent fuming, and those who speak openly, honestly, and effectively.

After watching dozens of couples, the two scholars predicted relationship outcomes and tracked their research subjects' relationships for the next ten years. Sure enough, they had predicted nearly 90 percent of the divorces that occurred.[2] Over time, couples who found a way to state their opinions about high-stakes, controversial, and emotional issues honestly and respectfully remained together. Those who didn't, split up.

Now, what about you? Think of your own important relationships. Are there a few crucial conversations that you're currently avoiding or handling poorly? Do you walk away from some issues only to come charging back into others? Do you hold in ugly opinions only to have them tumble out as sarcastic remarks or cheap shots? How about your significant other or family members? Are they constantly toggling from seething silence to subtle but costly attacks? When it matters the most (after all, these are your cherished loved ones), are you on your worst behavior? If so, you definitely have something to gain by learning more about how to handle crucial conversations.

Revitalize Your Community

Next, let's look at our neighborhoods and communities. If the fate of an organization is largely determined by how pivotal conversations are habitually handled, why should the communities that surround them be any different? The truth is, they aren't.

The difference between the *best* communities and the *good* or the *worst* is not the number of problems they have. All communities face problems. Once again, the difference lies in *how* they deal with problems. In the best communities, key individuals and groups find a way to engage in healthy dialogue. They talk through important issues. In contrast, communities that fail to improve play costly games. During community meetings people insult one another, become indignant, and act as if individuals with differing views are sick or deranged. Battles ensue.

In addition to how people behave in public forums, private behavior affects community health as well. Take, for example, the problem of crime. You might be shocked to discover a rather tragic statistic. Not everyone in prison is a career criminal who was born into a horrible family, then shaped by abuse and neglect into a seething sociopath. In fact, over half of the people who are convicted of violent crimes are *first-time offenders who commit crimes against friends or loved ones.*[3]

How could this be? Violence is often preceded by prolonged periods of silence. Most inmates once held a job, paid their bills, and remembered their friends' birthdays. Then one day, after allowing unresolved problems to build up and then boil over, they attacked a friend, loved one, or neighbor. That's right, convicted first-time offenders are often not career criminals. They're our frustrated neighbors. Since they don't know what to say or how to say it, they opt for force. In this case, the inability to work through tough issues devastates individuals, ruins families, and poisons communities.

What about where you live? What crucial issues does your community face? Are there conversations that people are not holding or not holding well that keep you from progress? Is crime skyrocketing? Do your community meetings look more like the *Jerry Springer* show than an energetic forum for healthy communication? If so, both you and the community have a lot to gain by focusing on how you handle high-stakes discussions.

Improve Your Personal Health

If the evidence so far isn't compelling enough to focus your attention on crucial conversations, what would you say if we told you that the ability to master high-stakes discussions is a key to a healthier and longer life?

Immune systems. Consider the groundbreaking research done by Dr. Janice Kiecolt-Glaser and Dr. Ronald Glaser. They studied the immune systems of couples who had been married an average of forty-two years by comparing those who argued constantly with those who resolved their differences effectively. It turns out that arguing for decades *doesn't* lessen the destructive blow of constant conflict. Quite the contrary. Those who routinely failed their crucial conversations had far weaker immune systems than those who found a way to resolve them well.[4] Of course, the weaker the immune system, the worse their health.

Life-threatening diseases. In perhaps the most revealing of all the health-related studies, a group of subjects who had contracted malignant melanoma received traditional treatment and then were divided into two groups. One group met weekly for only six weeks; the other did not. Facilitators taught the first group of recovering patients specific communication skills. (When it's your life that's at stake, could anything be *more* crucial?)

After meeting only six times and then dispersing for five years, the subjects who learned how to express themselves effectively had a higher survival rate—only 9 percent succumbed as opposed to almost 30 percent in the untrained group.[5] Think about the implications of this study. Just a modest improvement in ability to talk and connect with others corresponded to a two-thirds decrease in the death rate.

We could go on for pages about how the ability to hold crucial conversations has an impact on your personal health. The evidence is mounting every day. Nevertheless, most people find this claim a bit over the top. "Come on," they chide. "You're saying that the way you talk or don't talk affects your body? It could kill you?"

The short answer is yes. The longer answer suggests that the negative feelings we hold in, the emotional pain we suffer, and the constant battering we endure as we stumble our way through unhealthy conversations slowly eat away at our health. In some cases the impact of failed conversations leads to minor problems. In others it results in disaster. In all cases, failed conversations never make us happier, healthier, or better off.

So how about you? What are the specific conversations that gnaw at you the most? Which conversations (if you held them or improved them) would strengthen your immune system, help ward off disease, and increase your quality of life and well-being?

SUMMARY

When stakes are high, opinions vary, and emotions start to run strong, casual conversations become crucial. Ironically, the more crucial the conversation, the less likely we are to handle it well. The consequences of either avoiding or fouling up crucial conversations can be severe. When we fail a crucial conversation, every aspect of our lives can be affected—from our careers, to our communities, to our relationships, to our personal health.

As we learn how to step up to crucial conversations—and handle them well—with one set of skills we can influence virtually every domain of our lives.

What is this all-important skill-set? What do people who sail through crucial conversations actually do? More importantly, can we do it too?

2

Mastering Crucial Conversations

The Power of Dialogue

We (the authors) didn't always spend our time noodling over crucial conversations. In fact, we started our research into organizational and personal excellence by studying a slightly different topic. We figured that if we could learn why certain people were more effective than others, then we could learn exactly what they did, clone it, and pass it on to others.

To find the source of success, we started at work. We asked people to identify who they thought were their most effective colleagues. In fact, over the past twenty-five years, we've asked over twenty thousand people to identify the individuals in their organizations who could really get things done. We wanted to find those who were not just influential, but who were far more influential than the rest.

Each time, as we compiled the names into a list, a pattern emerged. Some people were named by one or two colleagues. Some found their way onto the lists of five or six people. These were the *good* at influence, but not good enough to be widely identified as top performers. And then there were the handful who were named thirty or more times. These were the *best*—the clear opinion leaders in their areas. Some were managers and supervisors. Many were not.

One of the opinion leaders we became particularly interested in meeting was named Kevin. He was the only one of eight vice presidents in his company to be identified as exceedingly influential. We wanted to know why. So we watched him at work.

At first, Kevin didn't do anything remarkable. In truth, he looked like every other VP. He answered his phone, talked to his direct reports, and continued about his pleasant, but routine, routine.

The Startling Discovery

After trailing Kevin for almost a week, we began to wonder if he really did act in ways that set him apart from others or if his influence was simply a matter of popularity. And then we followed Kevin into a meeting.

Kevin, his peers, and their boss were deciding on a new location for their offices—would they move across town, across the state, or across the country? The first two execs presented their arguments for their top choices, and as expected, their points were greeted by penetrating questions from the full team. No vague claim went unclarified, no unsupported reasoning unquestioned.

Then Chris, the CEO, pitched his preference—one that was both unpopular and potentially disastrous. However, when people tried to disagree or push back on Chris, he responded poorly. Since he was the big boss, he didn't exactly have to browbeat people to get what he wanted. Instead, he became slightly defensive. First he raised an eyebrow. Then he raised his finger. Finally he raised his voice—just a little. It wasn't long until people stopped questioning him, and Chris's inadequate proposal was quietly accepted.

Well almost. That's when Kevin spoke up. His words were simple enough—something like, "Hey Chris, can I check something out with you?"

The reaction was stunning—everyone in the room stopped breathing. But Kevin ignored the apparent terror of his colleagues and plunged on ahead. In the next few minutes he in essence told the CEO that he appeared to be violating his own decision-making guidelines. He was subtly using his power to move the new offices to his hometown.

Kevin continued to explain what he saw happening, and when he finished the first crucial minutes of this delicate exchange, Chris was quiet for a moment. Then he nodded his head. "You're absolutely right," he finally concluded. "I have been trying to force my opinion on you. Let's back up and try again."

This was a crucial conversation, and Kevin played no games whatsoever. He didn't resort to silence like his colleagues, nor did he try to force his arguments on others. As a result, the team chose a far more reasonable location and Kevin's boss appreciated his candor.

When Kevin was done, one of his peers turned to us and said, "Did you see how he did that? If you want to know how he gets things done, figure out what he just did."

So we did. In fact, we spent the next twenty-five years discovering what Kevin and people like him do. What typically set them apart from the rest of the pack was their ability to deal with crucial conversations. When talking turned tough and stakes were high, they excelled. But how? Kevin wasn't *that* different. He did step up to a tough issue and help the team make a better choice, but what exactly did he do? Did he possess learnable skills, or was what he did more magical than manageable?

To answer these questions, first, let's explore what Kevin was able to *achieve*. This will help us see where we're trying to go. Then we'll examine the dialogue tools effective communicators routinely use and learn to apply them to our own crucial conversations.

THE "ONE THING"

If you've seen the movie *City Slickers*, you may remember a scene where the crusty character Curly explains that if you want to succeed in life you have to do *one thing*. Then, in typical Hollywood fashion, he explains that he's not about to tell you what that one thing is. You have to figure it out yourself.

We won't pull a Curly. We'll reveal the one thing. When it comes to risky, controversial, and emotional conversations, skilled people find a way to get all relevant information (from themselves and others) out into the open.

That's it. At the core of every successful conversation lies the free flow of relevant information. People openly and honestly express their opinions, share their feelings, and articulate their theories. They willingly and capably share their views, even when their ideas are controversial or unpopular. It's the one thing, and it's precisely what Kevin and the other extremely effective communicators we studied were routinely able to achieve.

Now, to put a label on this spectacular talent—it's called dialogue.

> **di·a·logue** or **di·a·log** (dì´ ∂-lôg´´, -lòg) *n*
> The free flow of meaning between two or more people.

HERE'S HOW DIALOGUE WORKS

Despite the fact that we've shared the one thing, we're still left with two questions. First, how does this free flow of meaning lead to success? Second, what can you do to encourage meaning to flow freely?

We'll explain the relationship between the free flow of meaning and success right here and now. The second question—what you must do to stay in dialogue, no matter the circumstances—takes the rest of the book.

Filling the Pool of Shared Meaning

Each of us enters conversations with our own opinions, feelings, theories, and experiences about the topic at hand. This unique combination of thoughts and feelings makes up our personal pool of meaning. This pool not only informs us but also propels our every action.

When two or more of us enter *crucial* conversations, by definition we don't share the same pool. Our opinions differ. I believe one thing, you another. I have one history, you another.

People who are skilled at dialogue do their best to make it safe for everyone to add their meaning to the *shared* pool—even ideas that at first glance appear controversial, wrong, or at odds with their own beliefs. Now, obviously they don't agree with every idea; they simply do their best to ensure that all ideas find their way into the open.

As the Pool of Shared Meaning grows, it helps people in two ways. First, as individuals are exposed to more accurate and relevant information, they make better choices. In a very real sense, the Pool of Shared Meaning is a measure of a group's IQ. The larger the shared pool, the smarter the decisions. And even though many people may be involved in a choice, when people openly and freely share ideas, the increased time investment is more than offset by the quality of the decision.

On the other hand, we've all seen what happens when the shared pool is dangerously shallow. When people purposefully withhold meaning from one another, individually *smart* people can do collectively *stupid* things.

For example, a client of ours shared the following story.

A woman checked into the hospital to have a tonsillectomy, and the surgical team erroneously removed a portion of her foot. How could this tragedy happen? In fact, why is it that ninety-eight thousand hospital deaths each year stem from human error?[1] In part because many health-care professionals are afraid to speak their minds. In this case, no less than seven people wondered why the surgeon was working on the foot, but said nothing. Meaning didn't freely flow because people were afraid to speak up.

Of course, hospitals don't have a monopoly on fear. In every instance where bosses are smart, highly paid, confident, and outspoken (i.e., most of the world), people tend to hold back their opinions rather than risk angering someone in a position of power.

On the other hand, when people feel comfortable speaking up and meaning does flow freely, the shared pool can dramatically increase a group's ability to make better decisions. Consider what happened to Kevin's group. As everyone on the team began to explain his or her opinion, people formed a more clear and complete picture of the circumstances.

As they began to understand the whys and wherefores of different proposals, they built off one another. Eventually, as one idea led to the next, and then to the next, they came up with an alternative that no one had originally thought of and that all wholeheartedly supported. As a result of the free flow of meaning, the whole (final choice) was truly greater than the sum of the original parts. In short:

The Pool of Shared Meaning
is the birthplace of synergy.

Not only does a shared pool help individuals make better choices, but since the meaning is *shared*, people willingly act on whatever decisions they make. As people sit through an open discussion where ideas are shared, they take part in the free flow of meaning. Eventually they understand why the shared solution is the best solution, and they're committed to act. For example, Kevin and the other VPs didn't buy into their final choice simply because they were involved; they bought in because they understood.

Conversely, when people aren't involved, when they sit back quietly during touchy conversations, they're rarely committed to the final decision. Since their ideas remain in their heads and their opinions never make it into the pool, they end up quietly criticizing and passively resisting. Worse still, when others force their ideas into the pool, people have a harder time accepting the information. They may *say* they're on board, but then walk away and follow through halfheartedly. To quote Samuel Butler, "He that complies against his will is of his own opinion still."

The time you spend up front establishing a shared pool of meaning is more than paid for by faster, more committed action later on.

For example, if Kevin and the other leaders had not been committed to their relocation decision, terrible consequences would have followed. Some people would have agreed to move; others would have dragged their feet. Some would have held heated discussions in the hallways. Others would have said nothing and then quietly fought the plan. More likely than not, the team would have been forced to meet again, discuss again, and decide again—since only one person favored the decision and the decision affected everyone.

Now, don't get us wrong. We're not suggesting that every decision be made by consensus or that the boss shouldn't take part in or even make the final choice. We're simply suggesting that whatever the decision-making method, the greater the shared meaning in the pool, the better the choice—whoever makes it.

Every time we find ourselves arguing, debating, running away, or otherwise acting in an ineffective way, it's because we don't know how to share meaning. Instead of engaging in healthy dialogue, we play silly and costly games.

For instance, sometimes we move to silence. We play Salute and Stay Mute. That is, we don't confront people in positions of authority. Or at home we may play Freeze Your Lover. With this tortured technique we give loved ones the cold shoulder in order to get them to treat us better (what's the logic in that?).

Sometimes we rely on hints, sarcasm, innuendo, and looks of disgust to make our points. We play the martyr and then pretend we're actually trying to help. Afraid to confront an individual, we blame an entire team for a problem—hoping the message will hit the right target. Whatever the technique, the overall method is the same. We withhold meaning from the pool. We go to silence.

On other occasions, not knowing how to stay in dialogue, we rely on violence—anything from subtle manipulation to verbal attacks. We act like we know everything, hoping people will believe our arguments. We discredit others, hoping people won't believe their arguments. And then we use every manner of force to get our way. We borrow power from the boss; we hit people with biased monologues. The goal, of course, is always the same—to compel others to our point of view.

Now, here's how the various elements fit together. When stakes are high, opinions vary, and emotions run strong, we're often at our worst. In order to move to our best, we have to find a way to explain what is in each of our personal pools of meaning—

especially our high-stakes, sensitive, and controversial opinions, feelings, and ideas—and to get others to share their pools. We have to develop the tools that make it safe for us to discuss these issues and to come to a *shared* pool of meaning. And when we do, our lives change.

DIALOGUE SKILLS ARE LEARNABLE

And now for the *really* good news. The skills required to master high-stakes interactions are quite easy to spot and moderately easy to learn. First consider the fact that a well-handled crucial conversation all but leaps out at you. In fact, when you see someone enter the dangerous waters of a high-stakes, high-emotion, controversial discussion—and the person does a particularly good job—your natural reaction is to step back in awe. "Wow!" is generally the first word out of your mouth. What starts as a doomed discussion ends up with a healthy resolution. It can take your breath away.

More importantly, not only are dialogue skills easy to spot, but they're also fairly easy to learn. That's where we're going next. We've isolated and captured the skills of the dialogue-gifted through twenty-five years of nonstop "Wow!" research. First we followed around Kevin and dozens like him. Then, when conversations turned *crucial*, we took detailed notes. Afterward we compared our observations, tested our hypotheses, and honed our models until we found the skills that consistently explain the success of brilliant communicators. Finally, we combined our philosophies, theories, models, and skills into a package of learnable tools—tools for talking when stakes are high.

Now we're ready to share what we've learned. Stay with us as we explore how to transform crucial conversations from frightening events into interactions that yield success and results. It's the most important set of skills you'll ever master.

HERE'S WHERE WE'RE GOING

Here's what we'll focus on in the remainder of the book.

First, we'll explore the tools people use to help create the conditions of dialogue. The focus is on how we think about problem situations and what we do to prepare for them. As we work on ourselves, watch for problems, examine our own thought processes, discover our own styles, and then catch problems before they get out of hand, everyone benefits. As you read on, *you will learn how to create conditions in yourself and others that make dialogue the path of least resistance.*

Next, we'll examine the tools for talking, listening, and acting together. This is what most people have in mind when they think of crucial conversations. How do I express delicate feedback? How do I speak persuasively, not abrasively? And how about listening? Or better still, what can we do to get people to talk when they seem nervous? And how do we move from thought to action? As you read on, *you will learn the key skills of talking, listening, and acting together.*

Finally, we'll tie all of the theories and skills together by providing both a model and an extended example. Then, to see if you can really do what it takes, we provide seventeen situations that would give most of us fits—even people who are gifted at dialogue. As you read on, *you will master the tools for talking when stakes are high.*

3

Start with Heart

How to Stay Focused on What You Really Want

It's time to turn to the *how* of dialogue. How do you encourage the flow of meaning in the face of differing opinions and strong emotions? Given the average person's track record, it can't be all that easy. In fact, given most people's long-standing habit of costly behaviors, it'll probably require a lot of effort. The truth is, people *can* change. In fact, thousands of people we (the authors) have worked with over the past decades have made lasting improvements. But it requires work. You can't simply drink a magic potion and walk away renewed. Instead, you'll need to take a long hard look at yourself.

In fact, this is the first principle of dialogue—Start with Heart. That is, your *own* heart. If you can't get yourself right, you'll have a hard time getting dialogue right. When conversations become crucial you'll resort to the forms of communication that you've grown up with—debate, silent treatment, manipulation, and so on.

WHEN WE DON'T WORK ON ME FIRST

Let's start with a true story. Two young sisters and their father scurry into their hotel room after spending a hot afternoon at Disneyland. Given the repressive heat, the girls have consumed enough soda pop to fill a small barrel. As the two bursting kids enter their room, they have but one thought—to head for the head.

Since the bathroom is a one-holer, it isn't long until a fight breaks out. Both of the desperate children start arguing, pushing, and name-calling as they dance around the tiny bathroom. Eventually one calls out to her father for help.

"Dad, I got here first!"

"I know, but I need to go worse!"

"How do you know? You're not in my body. I didn't even go before we left this morning!"

"You're so selfish."

Dad proposes a plan. "Girls, I'm not going to solve this for you. You can stay in the bathroom and figure out who goes first and who goes second. There's only one rule. No hitting."

As the two antsy kids begin their crucial conversation, Dad checks his watch. He wonders how long it'll take. As the minutes slowly tick away, he hears nothing more than an occasional outburst of sarcasm. Finally after twenty-five long minutes, the toilet flushes. One girl comes out. A minute later, another flush and out walks her sister. With both girls in the room, Dad asks, "Do you know how many times both of you could have gone to the bathroom in the time it took you to work that out?"

The idea had not occurred to the little scamps, but the instant it does, it's obvious what both immediately conclude.

"Lots of times, if *she* hadn't been such a jerk."

"Listen to her. She's calling *me* names when *she* could have just waited. She always has to have her way!"

DON'T LOOK AT <u>ME</u>!

Laugh as we may at this story, these two kids behave no differently from the rest of us. When faced with a failed conversation, most of us are quick to blame others. If others would only change, then we'd all live happily ever after. If others weren't so screwed up, we wouldn't have to resort to silly games in the first place. They started it. It's their fault, not ours. And so on.

Although it's true that there are times when we are merely bystanders in life's never-ending stream of head-on collisions, rarely are we completely innocent. More often than not, we do something to contribute to the problems we're experiencing.

People who are best at dialogue understand this simple fact and turn it into the principle "Work on me first." They realize that not only are they likely to benefit by improving their own approach, but also that they're the only person they can work on anyway. As much as others may need to change, or we may *want* them to change, the only person we can continually inspire, prod, and shape—with any degree of success—is the person in the mirror.

There's a certain irony embedded in this fact. People who believe they need to start with themselves do just that. As they work on themselves, they also become the most skilled at dialogue. So here's the irony. It's the *most* talented, not the least talented, who are continually trying to improve their dialogue skills. As is often the case, the rich get richer.

START WITH HEART

Okay, let's assume we need to work on our own personal dialogue skills. Instead of buying this book and then handing it to a loved one or coworker and saying: "You'll love this, especially the parts that I've underlined for you," we'll try to figure out how we ourselves can benefit. But how? Where do we start? How can we stay clear of unhealthy games?

Although it's difficult to describe the specific order of events in an interaction as fluid as a crucial conversation, we do know one thing for certain: Skilled people Start with Heart. That is, they begin high-risk discussions with the right motives, and they stay focused no matter what happens.

They maintain this focus in two ways. First, they're steely-eyed smart when it comes to knowing what they want. Despite constant invitations to slip away from their goals, they stick with them. Second, skilled people don't make Sucker's Choices (either/or choices). Unlike others who justify their unhealthy behavior by explaining that they had no choice but to fight or take flight, the dialogue-smart believe that dialogue, no matter the circumstances, is always an option.

Let's look at each of these important heart-based assumptions in turn.

A MOMENT OF TRUTH

To see how the desires of our hearts can affect our ability to stay in dialogue, let's take a look at a real-life example.

Greta, the CEO of a mid-sized corporation, is two hours into a rather tense meeting with her top leaders. For the past six months she has been on a personal campaign to reduce costs. Little has been accomplished to date, so Greta calls the meeting. Surely people will tell her why they haven't started cutting costs. After all, she has taken great pains to foster candor.

Greta has just opened the meeting to questions when a manager haltingly rises to his feet, fidgets, stares at the floor, and then nervously asks if he can ask a very tough question. The way the fellow emphasizes the word *very* makes it sound as if he's about to accuse Greta of kidnapping the Lindbergh baby.

The frightened manager continues.

"Greta, you've been at us for six months to find ways to cut costs. I'd be lying if I said that we've given you much more than a lukewarm response. If you don't mind, I'd like to tell you about one thing that's making it tough for us to push for cost cuts."

"Great. Fire away," Greta says as she smiles in response.

"Well, while you've been asking us to use both sides of our paper and forego improvements, you're having a second office built."

Greta freezes and turns bright red. Everyone looks to see what will happen next. The manager plunges on ahead.

"The rumor is that the furniture alone will cost $150,000. Is that right?"

So there we have it. The conversation has just turned crucial. Someone has just poured a rather ugly tidbit into the pool of meaning. Will Greta continue to encourage honest feedback, or will she shut the fellow down?

We call this a crucial conversation because how Greta acts during the next few moments will not only set people's attitudes toward the proposed cost cutting, but will also have a huge impact on what the other leaders think about her. Does she walk the talk of openness and honesty? Or is she a raging hypocrite— like so many of the senior executives who came before her?

Will We Get Hooked?

How Greta behaves during this crucial conversation depends a great deal on how she handles her emotions while under attack. Sure, when she's giving a speech or writing a memo, she's all for candor. She's a veritable cheerleader for candor. But what about now? Will Greta thank the fellow for taking a huge risk and being honest?

If she's like most of us, Greta will defend herself. When we're in the throes of high-stakes conversations, new (and less healthy) motives often supplant our original, more noble ones. If you are standing in front of a potentially hostile crowd, it's a good bet you will change your original goal to the new goal of protecting your public image.

"Excuse me," you might respond. "I don't think that my new office is an appropriate topic for this forum."

Bang. You're dead. In one fell swoop you've lost buy-in, destroyed any hope for candor in this particular conversation, and confirmed everyone's suspicion that you want honesty—but only as long as it makes you look good.

FIRST, FOCUS ON WHAT YOU <u>REALLY</u> WANT

In reality, Greta didn't give in to her raging desire to defend herself. After being accused of not following her own advice, at first she looked surprised, embarrassed, and maybe even a little upset. Then she took a deep breath and said: "You know what? We need to talk about this. I'm glad you asked the question. It'll give us a chance to discuss what's really going on."

And then Greta talked turkey. She explained that she felt the office was necessary but admitted that she had no idea what it would cost. So she sent someone to check the numbers. Meanwhile, she explained that building the office was a response to marketing's advice to boost the company's image and improve client confidence. And while Greta *would* use the office, it would be primarily a hosting location for marketing. When she saw the figures for the office, Greta was stunned and admitted that she should have checked the costs before signing a work order. So then and there she committed to drawing up a new plan that would cut costs by half or canceling the project entirely.

Later that day we asked Greta how she had been able to keep her composure under fire. We wanted to know exactly what had been going on in her head. What had helped her move from embarrassment and anger to gratitude?

"It was easy," Greta explained. "At first I did feel attacked, and I wanted to strike back. To be honest, I wanted to put that guy in his place. He was accusing me in public and he was wrong."

"And then it struck me," she continued. "Despite the fact that I had four hundred eyeballs pinned to me, a rather important question hit me like a ton of bricks: 'What do I *really* want here?'"

Asking this question had a powerful effect on Greta's thinking. As she focused on this far more important question, she quickly realized that her goal was to encourage these two hundred managers to embrace the cost-reduction efforts—and to thereby influence thousands of others to do the same.

As Greta contemplated this goal, she realized that the biggest barrier she faced was the widespread belief that she was a hypocrite. On the one hand, she was calling for others to sacrifice. On the other, she appeared to be spending discretionary funds for her own comfort. It was at that moment that she was no longer ashamed or angry, but grateful. She couldn't have asked for a better opportunity to influence these leaders than the one offered up by this penetrating question. And so she moved to dialogue.

Refocus your brain. Now, let's move to a situation you might face. You're speaking with someone who completely disagrees with you on a hot issue. How does all of this goal stuff apply? As you begin the discussion, start by examining your motives. Going in, ask yourself what you really want.

Also, as the conversation unfolds and you find yourself starting to, say, defer to the boss or give your spouse the cold shoulder, pay attention to what's happening to your objectives. Are you starting to change your goal to save face, avoid embarrassment, win, be right, or punish others? Here's the tricky part. Our motives usually change without any conscious thought on our part. When adrenaline does our thinking for us, our motives flow with the chemical tide.

In order to move back to motives that allow for dialogue, you must step away from the interaction and look at yourself—much like an outsider. Ask yourself: "What am I doing, and if I had to guess, what does it tell me about my underlying motive?" As you make an honest effort to discover your motive, you might conclude: "Let's see. I'm pushing hard, making the argument stronger than I actually believe, and doing anything to win. I've shifted from trying to select a vacation location to trying to win an argument."

Once you call into question the shifting desires of your heart, you can make conscious choices to change them. "What I really want is to genuinely try to select a vacation spot we can all enjoy—rather than try to win people over to my ideas." Put succinctly, when you name the game, you can stop playing it.

But how? How do you recognize what has happened to you, stop playing games, and then influence your own motives? Do what Greta did. Stop and ask yourself some questions that return you to dialogue. You can ask these questions either when you find yourself slipping out of dialogue or as reminders when you prepare to step up to a crucial conversation. Here are some great ones:

What do I really want for myself?

What do I really want for others?

What do I really want for the relationship?

Once you've asked yourself what you want, add one more equally telling question:

How would I behave if I really wanted these results?

Find your bearings. There are two good reasons for asking these questions. First, the answer to what we really want helps us to locate our own North Star. Despite the fact that we're being tempted to take the wrong path by (1) people who are trying to pick a fight, (2) thousands of years of genetic hardwiring that brings our emotions to a quick boil, and (3) our deeply ingrained habit of trying to win, our North Star returns us to our original purpose.

> "What do I really want? Oh yeah, I guess it's not to make the other person squirm or to preen in front of a crowd. I want people to freely and openly talk about what it'll take to cut costs."

Take charge of your body. The second reason for asking what we *really* want is no less important. When we ask ourselves what we really want, we affect our entire physiology. As we introduce complex and abstract questions to our mind, the problem-solving part of our brain recognizes that we are now dealing with intricate social issues and not physical threats. When we present our brain with a demanding question, our body sends precious blood to the parts of our brain that help us think, and away from the parts of our body that help us take flight or begin a fight.

Asking questions about what we really want serves two important purposes. First, it reminds us of our goal. Second, it juices up our brain in a way that helps us keep focused.

Common Deviations

As we step up to a crucial conversation, fully intending to stimulate the flow of meaning, many of us quickly change our original objectives to much less healthy goals. For instance, when Greta fell under public attack, her immediate reaction was to do whatever it took to save face. Other common, but not-all-that-healthy, objectives include wanting to win, seeking revenge, and hoping to remain safe.

Wanting to win. This particular dialogue killer sits at the top of many of our lists. Heaven only knows that we come by this deadly passion naturally enough. Half of the TV programs we watch make heroes out of people who win at sports or game shows. Ten minutes into kindergarten we learn that if we want to get the teacher's attention, we have to spout the right answer. That means we have to beat our fellow students at the same game. This desire to win is built into our very fiber before we're old enough to know what's going on.

Unfortunately, as we grow older, most of us don't realize that this desire to win is continually driving us away from healthy dialogue. We start out with the goal of resolving a problem, but as soon as someone raises the red flag of inaccuracy or challenges our correctness, we switch purposes in a heartbeat.

First we correct the facts. We quibble over details and point out flaws in the other person's arguments.

"You're wrong! We're not spending anywhere near a hundred and fifty thousand dollars on the furniture. It's the redesign of the office that's costing so much, not the furniture."

Of course, as others push back, trying to prove their points, it's not long until we change our goal from correcting mistakes to winning.

If you doubt this simple allegation, think of the two antsy young girls as they stared each other down in the cramped bathroom. Their original goal was simple enough—relief. But soon, caught up in their own painful game, the two set their jaws and committed to doing whatever it took to win—even if it brought them a fair amount of personal discomfort.

Seeking revenge. Sometimes, as our anger increases, we move from wanting to win the point to wanting to harm the other person. Just ask Greta. "To heck with honest communication!" she thinks to herself. "I'll teach the moron not to attack me in public." Eventually, as emotions reach their peak, our goal becomes completely perverted. We move so far away from adding meaning to the pool that now all we want is to see others suffer.

> "I can't believe that you're accusing me of squandering good money on a perfectly fine office. Now, if nobody else has any intelligent questions, let's move on!"

Everyone immediately clams up and looks at the floor. The silence is deafening.

Hoping to remain safe. Of course, we don't always fix mistakes, aggressively discredit others, or heartlessly try to make them suffer. Sometimes we choose personal safety over dialogue. Rather than add to the pool of meaning, and possibly make waves along the way, we go to silence. We're so uncomfortable with the immediate conflict that we accept the *certainty* of bad results to avoid the *possibility* of uncomfortable conversation. We choose (at least in our minds) peace over conflict. Had this happened in Greta's case, nobody would have raised concerns over the new office, Greta never would have learned the real issue, and people would have continued to drag their feet.

SECOND, REFUSE THE SUCKER'S CHOICE

Now, let's add one more tool that helps us focus on what we really want. We'll start with a story.

The faculty of Beaumont High School is hashing out possible curriculum changes in an after-school meeting that's been going on for hours. It's finally the science department's turn to present.

Royce, a chemistry teacher who's been at Beaumont for

thirty-three years, considers himself the elder statesman of the school. He's much more fond of war stories than he is of neutrons and electrons, but the administration kind of turns a blind eye, because the guy's a fixture.

At the principal's cue, Royce clears his throat and begins to yammer on incoherently about the similarities between curriculum development and battle preparations. His antics are so embarrassing that the audience quietly heaves their shoulders as they futilely try to stifle their laughter.

Next, it's Brent's, the new guy's, turn. A couple of weeks ago, the principal asked him to outline the science department's proposed curriculum changes. Brent met with his colleagues (even Royce), gathered suggestions, and came ready to present.

As Brent begins, Royce starts demonstrating bayonet offensives with a yardstick, and Brent snaps. Slamming his fist on the table, he shouts, "Am I the only one who wonders why we even allow this fosil to talk? Did he miss a pill or something?"

A room full of stunned faces turns toward Brent. Realizing that his colleagues must think he's possessed, Brent utters those words we've all come to hate, "Hey, don't look at me like that! I'm the only one around who has the guts to speak the truth."

What a tactic. Brent slams Royce in public, and then instead of apologizing or maybe simply fading into the shadows, he argues that what he just did was somehow noble.

Two ugly options. This pernicious strategy is particularly well suited for keeping us off track. It's known as a Sucker's Choice. In order to justify an especially sordid behavior, we suggest that we're caught between two distasteful options. Either we can be honest and attack our spouse, or we can be kind and withhold the truth. Either we can disagree with the boss to help make a better choice—and get shot for it—or we can remain quiet, starve the pool, and keep our job. Pick your poison.

What makes these *Sucker's* Choices is that they're always set up as the only two options available. It's the worst of either/or thinking. The person making the choice never suggests there's a third option that doesn't call for unhealthy behavior. For example, maybe there's a way to be honest *and* respectful. Perhaps we can express our candid opinion to our boss *and* be safe.

Those offering up a Sucker's Choice either don't think of a third (and healthy) option—in which case it's an honest but tragic mistake—or set up the false dichotomy as a way of justifying their unattractive actions. "I'm sorry, but I just had to destroy the guy's self-image if I was going to keep my integrity. It wasn't pretty, but it was the right thing to do."

Open Yourself to Change

Not only do Sucker's Choices set us up to take ineffective actions, but they close us down to change. They present our brain with problems easily solved with restricted blood flow. After all, if we are simply choosing between fight and flight, who needs much creative thought?

They also keep us stuck in ineffective strategies by justifying our attacking or retreating behaviors. Why alter our behavior when we're the only one savvy enough to keep quiet? "Stand up to my boss? What turnip wagon did you just fall off?" "Tell my spouse that her parental style is too controlling? No way. I'll pay for years." In a similar vein, why would you ever change when you think you're the only one around with an ounce of integrity? "Somebody has to state the ugly truth. It's the only way I can look myself in the mirror."

In summary, Sucker's Choices are simplistic tradeoffs that keep us from thinking creatively of ways to get to dialogue, and that justify our silly games.

So how do we break away from perverted logic that keeps us trapped in hurtful behavior?

Search for the Elusive <u>And</u>

The *best* at dialogue refuse Sucker's Choices by setting up new choices. They present themselves with tougher questions— questions that turn the either/or choice into a search for the all-important and ever-elusive *and*. (It is an endangered species, you know.) Here's how this works.

First, clarify what you really *want.* You've got a head start if you've already Started with Heart. If you know what you want for yourself, for others, and for the relationship, then you're in position to break out of the Sucker's Choice.

> "What I want is for my husband to be more reliable. I'm tired of being let down by him when he makes commitments that I depend on."

Second, clarify what you really don't *want.* This is the key to framing the *and* question. Think of what you are afraid will happen to you if you back away from your current strategy of trying to win or stay safe. What bad thing will happen if you stop pushing so hard? Or if you don't try to escape? What horrible outcome makes game-playing an attractive and sensible option?

> "What I don't want is to have a useless and heated conversation that creates bad feelings and doesn't lead to change."

Third, present your brain with a more complex problem. Finally, combine the two into an *and* question that forces you to search for more creative and productive options than silence and violence.

"How can I have a candid conversation with my husband about being more dependable and avoid creating bad feelings or wasting our time?"

It's interesting to watch what happens when people are presented with *and* questions after being stuck with Sucker's Choices. Their faces become reflective, their eyes open wider, and they begin to *think*. With surprising regularity, when people are asked: "Is it possible that there's a way to accomplish both?" they acknowledge that there very well may be.

Is there a way to tell your peer your real concerns *and* not insult or offend him?

Is there a way to talk to your neighbors about their annoying behavior *and* not come across as self-righteous or demanding?

Is there a way to talk with your loved one about how you're spending money *and* not get into an argument?

IS THIS REALLY POSSIBLE?

Some people find this whole line of thinking comically unrealistic. From their point of view, Sucker's Choices aren't false dichotomies; they're merely a reflection of an unfortunate reality.

"You can't say something to the boss about our upcoming move. It'll cost you your job."

To these people we say: Remember Kevin? He, and almost every other opinion leader we've ever studied, has what it takes to speak up *and* maintain respect. Maybe you don't know what Kevin did or what you need to do—but don't deny the existence of Kevin or people like him. There is a third set of options out there that allows you to add meaning to the pool *and* build on the relationship.

When we (the authors) are in the middle of an on-site workshop and we suggest there are alternatives to Sucker's Choices, someone invariably says: "Maybe you can speak honestly and still be heard in other organizations, but if you try it here, you'll be eaten alive!" Or the flip side: "You've got to know when to fold if you want to survive for another day." Then in a hail of "I'll say!" and "Here, here!" many nod in agreement.

At first, we thought that maybe there *were* places where dialogue couldn't survive. But then we learned to ask: "Are you saying there isn't *anyone* you know who is able to hold a high-risk conversation in a way that solves problems *and* builds relationships?" There usually is.

SUMMARY—START WITH HEART

Here's how people who are skilled at dialogue stay focused on their goals—particularly when the going gets tough.

Work on Me First

- Remember that the only person you can directly control is yourself.

Focus on What You <u>Really</u> Want

- When you find yourself moving toward silence or violence, stop and pay attention to your motives.

  - Ask yourself: "What does my behavior tell me about what my motives are?"

  - Then, clarify what you *really* want. Ask yourself: "What do I want for myself? For others? For the relationship?"

  - And finally, ask: "How would I behave if this were what I really wanted?"

Refuse the Sucker's Choice

- As you consider what you want, notice when you start talking yourself into a Sucker's Choice.

  - Watch to see if you're telling yourself that you must choose between peace and honesty, between winning and losing, and so on.

  - Break free of these Sucker's Choices by searching for the *and*.

  - Clarify what you don't want, add it to what you do want, and ask your brain to start searching for healthy options to bring you to dialogue.

4

Learn to Look

How to Notice When Safety Is at Risk

Let's start this chapter by visiting a crucial conversation. You've just ended a heated debate with a group of people you supervise. What started out as a harmless discussion about your new shift rotations ended up as a nasty argument. After an hour of carping and complaining, you finally went to your separate corners.

You're now walking down the hall wondering what happened. In a matter of minutes an innocent discussion had transformed into a crucial conversation, and then into a *failed* conversation—and you can't recall why. You do remember a tense moment when you started pushing your point of view a bit too hard (okay, maybe *way* too hard) and eight people stared at you as if you had just bitten the head off a chicken. But then the meeting ended.

What you don't realize is that two of your friends are walking down the hallway in the opposite direction conducting a play-by-play of the meeting. They *do* know what took place.

"It happened again. The boss started pushing so hard for personal agenda items that we all began to act defensively. Did you notice how at one point all of our jaws dropped simultaneously? Of course, I was just as bad as the boss. I spoke in absolutes, only pointed out facts that supported my view, and then ended with a list of outlandish claims. I got hooked like a marlin."

Later that day as you talk to your friends about the meeting, they let you in on what happened. You were there, but somehow you missed what actually *happened*.

"That's because you were so caught up in the *content* of the conversation," your buddy explains. "You cared so deeply about the shift rotation that you were blind to the *conditions*. You know—how people were feeling and acting, what tone they were taking, stuff like that."

"You saw all that while still carrying on a heated conversation?" you ask.

"Yeah," your coworker explains, "I always dual-process. That is, when things start turning ugly, I watch the content of the conversation along with what people are doing. I look for and examine both *what* and *why*. If you can see why people are becoming upset or holding back their views or even going silent, you can do something to get back on track."

"You look at the 'conditions,' and then you know what to do to get back on track?"

"Sometimes," your friend answers. "But you've got to learn exactly what to look for."

"It's a form of social first aid. By watching for the moment a conversation starts turning unhealthy, you can respond quickly. The sooner you catch a problem, the sooner you'll be able to work your way back to healthy dialogue, and the less severe the damage."

You can't believe how obvious this advice is—and yet you've never thought of such a thing. Weirder still, your friend has. In fact, he has a whole vocabulary for what's going on during a crucial conversation. It's as if you've been speaking another language.

WATCH FOR CONDITIONS

In truth, most of us do have trouble dual-processing (watching for content *and* conditions)—especially when it comes to a crucial conversation. When both stakes and emotions are high, we get so caught up in what we're saying that it can be nearly impossible to pull ourselves out of the argument in order to see what's happening to ourselves and to others. Even when we are startled by what's going on, enough so that we think: "Yipes! This has turned ugly. Now what?" we may not know what to look for in order to turn things around. We may not see enough of what's happening.

How could that be? How could we be smack-dab in the middle of a heated debate and not really see what's going on? A metaphor might help. It's akin to going fly fishing for the first time with an experienced angler. Your buddy keeps telling you to cast your fly six feet upstream from that brown trout "just out there." Only you can't see a brown trout "just out there." He can. That's because he knows what to look for. You *think* you do. You think you need to look for a brown trout. In reality, you need to look for a brown trout that's under water while the sun is reflecting in your eyes. You have to look for elements other than the thing that your dad has stuffed and mounted over the fireplace. It takes both knowledge and practice to know what to look for and then actually see it.

So what do you look for when caught in the middle of a crucial conversation? What do you need to see in order to catch problems before they become too severe? Actually, it helps to watch for three different conditions: the moment a conversation turns crucial, signs that people don't feel safe (silence or violence), and your own Style Under Stress. Let's consider each of these conversation killers in turn.

Learn to Spot Crucial Conversations

First, stay alert for the moment a conversation turns from a routine or harmless discussion into a crucial one. In a similar vein, as you anticipate entering a tough conversation, pay heed to the fact that you're about to enter the danger zone. Otherwise, you can easily get sucked into silly games before you realize what's happened. And as we suggested earlier, the further you stray off track, the harder it can be to return.

To help catch problems early, reprogram your mind to pay attention to the signs that suggest you're in a crucial conversation. Some people first notice *physical* signals—their stomach gets tight or their eyes get dry. Think about what happens to your body when conversations get tough. Everyone is a little bit different. What are your cues? Whatever they are, learn to look at them as signs to step back, slow down, and Start with Heart before things get out of hand.

Others notice their *emotions* before they notice signs in their body. They realize they are scared, hurt, or angry and are beginning to react to or suppress these feelings. These emotions can also be great cues to tell you to step back, slow down, and take steps to turn your brain back on.

Some people's first cue is not physical or emotional, but *behavioral*. It's like an out-of-body experience. They see themselves raising their voice, pointing their finger like a loaded weapon, or becoming very quiet. It's only then that they realize how they're feeling.

So take a moment to think about some of your toughest conversations. What cues can you use to recognize that your brain is beginning to disengage and you're at risk of moving away from healthy dialogue?

Learn to Look for Safety Problems

If you can catch signs that the conversation is starting to turn crucial—before you get sucked so far into the actual argument that you can never withdraw from the content—then you can start dual-processing immediately. And what exactly should you watch for? People who are gifted at dialogue keep a constant vigil on safety. They pay attention to the content—that's a given—and they watch for signs that people are afraid. When friends, loved ones, or colleagues move away from healthy dialogue (freely adding to the pool of meaning)—either forcing their opinions into the pool or purposefully keeping their ideas out of the pool—they immediately turn their attention to whether or not others feel safe.

When it's safe, you can say anything. Here's why gifted communicators keep a close eye on safety. Dialogue calls for the free flow of meaning—period. And nothing kills the flow of meaning like fear. When you fear that people aren't buying into your ideas, you start pushing too hard. When you fear that you may be harmed in some way, you start withdrawing and hiding. Both these reactions—to fight and to take flight—are motivated by the same emotion: fear. On the other hand, if you make it safe enough, you can talk about almost anything and people will listen. If you don't fear that you're being attacked or humiliated, you yourself can hear almost anything and not become defensive.

Think about your own experience. Can you remember receiving really blistering feedback from someone at some point in your life, but in this instance you didn't become defensive? Instead, you absorbed the feedback. You reflected on it. You allowed it to influence you. If so, ask yourself why. Why in this instance were you able to absorb potentially threatening feedback so well? If you're like the rest of us, it's because you believed that the other person had your best interest in mind. In addition, you respected the other person's opinion. You felt *safe* receiving the feedback because you trusted the motives and ability of the other person. You didn't need to defend yourself from what was being said.

On the other hand, if you don't feel safe, you can't take any feedback. It's as if the pool of meaning has a lid on it. "What do you mean I look good? Is that some kind of joke? Are you ribbing me?" When you don't feel safe, even well-intended comments are suspect.

When it's unsafe, you start to go blind. By carefully watching for safety violations, not only can you see when dialogue is in danger, but you can also reengage your brain. As we've said before, when your emotions start cranking up, key brain functions start shutting down. Not only do you prepare to take flight, but your peripheral vision actually narrows. In fact, when you feel genuinely threatened, you can scarcely see beyond what's right in front of you. Similarly, when you feel the outcome of a conversation is being threatened, you have a hard time seeing beyond the point you're trying to make. By pulling yourself out of the content of an argument and watching for fear, you reengage your brain and your full vision returns.

Don't let safety problems lead you astray. Let's add a note of caution. When others begin to feel unsafe, they start doing nasty things. Now, since they're feeling unsafe, you should be thinking to yourself: "Hey, they're feeling unsafe. I need to do something—maybe make it safer." That's what you *should* be thinking. Unfortunately, since others feel unsafe, they may be trying to make fun of you, insult you, or bowl you over with their arguments. This kind of aggressive behavior doesn't exactly bring out the diplomat in you. So instead of taking their attack as a sign that safety is at risk, you take it at its face—as an attack. "I'm under attack!" you think. Then you respond in kind. Or maybe you try to escape. Either way you're not dual-processing and then pulling out a skill to restore safety. Instead, you're becoming part of the problem as you get pulled into the fight.

Imagine the magnitude of what we're suggesting here. We're asking you to recode silence and violence as signs that people are feeling unsafe. We're asking you to fight your natural tendency to respond in kind. We're asking you to undo years of practice, maybe even eons of genetic shaping that prod you to take flight or pick a fight (when under attack), and recode the stimulus. "Ah, that's a sign that the other person feels unsafe." And then what? Do something to make it safe. In the next chapter we'll explore how. For now, simply learn to look for safety and then be curious, not angry or frightened.

Silence and Violence

As people begin to feel unsafe, they start down one of two unhealthy paths. They move either to silence (withholding meaning from the pool) or to violence (trying to force meaning in the pool). That part we know. But let's add a little more detail. Just as a little knowledge of what to look for can turn blurry water into a brown trout, knowing a few of the common forms of silence and violence helps you see safety problems when they first start to happen. That way you can step out, restore safety, and return to dialogue—before the damage is too great.

Silence

Silence consists of any act to purposefully withhold information from the pool of meaning. It's almost always done as a means of avoiding potential problems, and it always restricts the flow of meaning. Methods range from playing verbal games to avoiding a person entirely. The three most common forms of silence are masking, avoiding, and withdrawing.

- *Masking* consists of understating or selectively showing our true opinions. Sarcasm, sugarcoating, and couching are some of the more popular forms.

"I think your idea is, uh, brilliant. Yeah, that's it. I just worry that others won't catch the subtle nuances. Some ideas come before their time, so expect some, uh, minor resistance."

Meaning: Your idea is insane, and people will fight it with their last breath.

"Oh yeah, that'll work like a charm. Offer people a discount, and they'll drive all the way across town just to save six cents on a box of soap. Where do you come up with this stuff?"

Meaning: What a dumb idea.

- *Avoiding* involves steering completely away from sensitive subjects. We talk, but without addressing the real issues.

"How does your new suit look? Well, you know that blue's my favorite color."

Meaning: What happened? Did you buy your clothes at the circus?

"Speaking of ideas for cost cutting—did you see Friends *last night? Joey inherited a bunch of money and was buying stupid stuff. It was a hoot."*

Meaning: Let's not talk about how to cut costs. It always leads to a fight.

- *Withdrawing* means pulling out of a conversation altogether. We either exit the conversation or exit the room.

"Excuse me. I've got to take this call."

Meaning: I'd rather gnaw off my own arm than spend one more minute in this useless meeting.

"Sorry, I'm not going to talk about how to split up the phone bill again. I'm not sure our friendship can stand another battle." (Exits.)

Meaning: We can't talk about even the simplest of topics without arguing.

Violence

Violence consists of any verbal strategy that attempts to convince, control, or compel others to your point of view. It violates safety by trying to force meaning into the pool. Methods range from name-calling and monologuing to making threats. The three most common forms are controlling, labeling, and attacking.

- *Controlling* consists of coercing others to your way of thinking. It's done through either forcing your views on others or dominating the conversation. Methods include cutting others off, overstating your facts, speaking in absolutes, changing subjects, or using directive questions to control the conversation.

  "There's not a person in the world who hasn't bought one of these things. They're the perfect gift."

  Meaning: I can't justify spending our hard-earned savings on this expensive toy, but I really want it.

  "We tried their product, but it was an absolute disaster. Everyone knows that they can't deliver on time and that they offer the worst customer service on the planet."

  Meaning: I'm not certain of the real facts so I'll use hyperbole to get your attention.

- *Labeling* is putting a label on people or ideas so we can dismiss them under a general stereotype or category.

  "Your ideas are practically Neanderthal. Any thinking person would follow my plan."

Meaning: I can't argue my case on its merits.

"You're not going to listen to them are you? For crying out loud! First, they're from headquarters. Second, they're engineers. Need I say more?"

Meaning: If I pretend that all people from headquarters and all engineers are somehow bad and wrong, I won't have to explain anything.

- *Attacking* speaks for itself. You've moved from winning the argument to making the person suffer. Tactics include belittling and threatening.

"Try that stupid little stunt and see what happens."

Meaning: I will get my way on this even if I have to bad-mouth you and threaten some vague punishment.

"Don't listen to a word Jim is saying. I'm sorry Jim, but I'm on to you. You're just trying to make it better for your team while making the rest of us suffer. I've seen you do it before. You're a real jerk, you know that? I'm sorry, but someone has to have the guts to tell it like it is."

Meaning: To get my way I'll say bad things about you and then pretend that I'm the only one with any integrity.

Look for Your Style Under Stress

Let's say you've been watching for both content and conditions. You're paying special attention to when a conversation turns crucial. To catch this important moment, you're looking for signs that safety is at risk. As safety is violated, you even know to watch for various forms of silence and violence. So are you now fully armed? Have you seen all there is to see?

Actually, no. Perhaps the most difficult element to watch closely as you're madly dual-processing is your own behavior.

Frankly, most people have trouble pulling themselves away from the tractor beam of the argument at hand. Then you've got the problem other people present as they employ all kinds of tactics. You've got to watch them like a hawk. It's little wonder that paying close attention to your own behavior tends to take a backseat. Besides, it's not like you can actually step out of your body and observe yourself. You're on the wrong side of your eyeballs.

Low self-monitors. The truth is, we all have trouble monitoring our own behavior at times. We usually lose any semblance of social sensitivity when we become so consumed with ideas and causes that we lose track of what we're doing. We try to bully our way through. We speak when we shouldn't. We do things that don't work—all in the name of a cause. We eventually become so unaware that we become a bit like this fellow of Jack Handy's invention.

> "People were always talking about how mean this guy was who lived on our block. But I decided to go see for myself. I went to his door, but he said he wasn't the mean guy, the mean guy lived in that house over there. 'No, you stupid idiot,' I said, 'that's my house.'"

Unfortunately, when you fail to monitor your own behavior, you can look pretty silly. For example, you're talking to your spouse about the fact that he or she left you sitting at the auto repair shop for over an hour. After pointing out that it was a simple misunderstanding, your spouse exclaims: "You don't have to get angry."

Then you utter those famous words: "I'm not angry!"

Of course, you're spraying spit as you shout out your denial, and the vein on your forehead has swelled to the size of a teenage python. You, quite naturally, don't see the inconsistency in your response. You're in the middle of the whole thing, and you don't appreciate it one bit when your spouse laughs at you.

You also play this denial game when you ingenuously answer the question, "What's wrong?"

"Nothing's wrong," you whimper. Then you shuffle your feet, stare at the floor, and look wounded.

Become a Vigilant Self-Monitor

What does it take to be able to step out of an argument and watch for process—including what you yourself are doing and the impact you're having? You have to become a vigilant self-monitor. That is, pay close attention to what you're doing and the impact it's having, and then alter your strategy if necessary. Specifically, watch to see if you're having a good or bad impact on safety.

Your Style Under Stress Test

What kind of a self-monitor are you? One good way to increase your self-awareness is to explore your Style Under Stress. What do you do when talking turns tough? To find out, fill out the survey on the following pages. Or, for easier scoring, visit www.crucialconversations.com/sus. It'll help you see what tactics you typically revert to when caught in the midst of a crucial conversation. It'll also help you determine which parts of this book can be most helpful to you.

Instructions. The following questions explore how you *typically* respond when you're in the middle of a crucial conversation. Before answering, pick a specific relationship at work or at home. Then answer the items while thinking about how you typically approach risky conversations in that relationship.

T   F   1. At times I avoid situations that might bring me into contact with people I'm having problems with.

T   F   2. I have put off returning phone calls or emails because I simply didn't want to deal with the person who sent them.

T   F   3. Sometimes when people bring up a touchy or awkward issue, I try to change the subject.

T   F   4. When it comes to dealing with awkward or stressful subjects, sometimes I hold back rather than give my full and candid opinion.

T   F   5. Rather than tell people exactly what I think, sometimes I rely on jokes, sarcasm, or snide remarks to let them know I'm frustrated.

T   F   6. When I've got something tough to bring up, sometimes I offer weak or insincere compliments to soften the blow.

T   F   7. In order to get my point across, I sometimes exaggerate my side of the argument.

T   F   8. If I seem to be losing control of a conversation, I might cut people off or change the subject in order to bring it back to where I think it should be.

T   F   9. When others make points that seem stupid to me, I sometimes let them know it without holding back at all.

T   F   10. When I'm stunned by a comment, sometimes I say things that others might take as forceful or attacking—comments such as "Give me a break!" or "That's ridiculous!"

T   F   11. Sometimes when things get heated, I move from arguing against others' points to saying things that might hurt them personally.

T   F   12. If I get into a heated discussion, I've been known to be tough on the other person. In fact, the person might feel a bit insulted or hurt.

T   F   13. When I'm discussing an important topic with others, sometimes I move from trying to make my point to trying to win the battle.

T   F   14. In the middle of a tough conversation, I often get so caught up in arguments that I don't see how I'm coming across to others.

T   F   15. When talking gets tough and I do something hurtful, I'm quick to apologize for mistakes.

T   F   16. When I think about a conversation that took a bad turn, I tend to focus first on what I did that was wrong rather than focus on others' mistakes.

T   F   17. When I've got something to say that others might not want to hear, I avoid starting out with tough conclusions, and instead start with facts that help them understand where I'm coming from.

T   F   18. I can tell very quickly when others are holding back or feeling defensive in a conversation.

T   F   19. Sometimes I decide that it's better not to give harsh feedback because I know that it's bound to cause real problems.

T   F   20. When conversations aren't working, I step back from the fray, think about what's happening, and take steps to make it better.

T   F   21. When others get defensive because they misunderstand me, I quickly get us back on track by clarifying what I do and don't mean.

T F 22. There are some people I'm rough on because, to be honest, they need or deserve what I give them.

T F 23. I sometimes make absolute statements like "The fact is . . ." or "It's obvious that . . ." to be sure I get my point across.

T F 24. If others hesitate to share their views, I sincerely invite them to say what's on their mind, no matter what it is.

T F 25. At times I argue hard for my view—hoping to keep others from bringing up opinions that would be a waste of energy to discuss.

T F 26. Even when things get tense, I adapt quickly to how others are responding to me and try a new strategy.

T F 27. When I find that I'm at cross-purposes with someone, I often keep trying to win my way rather than looking for common ground.

T F 28. When things don't go well, I'm more inclined to see the mistakes others made than notice my own role.

T F 29. After I share strong opinions, I go out of my way to invite others to share their views, particularly opposing ones.

T F 30. When others hesitate to share their views, I do whatever I can to make it safe for them to speak honestly.

T F 31. Sometimes I have to discuss things I thought had been settled because I don't keep track of what was discussed before.

T F   32. I find myself in situations where people get their feelings hurt because they thought they would have more of a say in final decisions than they end up having.

T F   33. I get frustrated sometimes at how long it takes some groups to make decisions because too many people are involved.

Style Under Stress Score

Please fill out the score sheets in Figures 4-1 and 4-2. Each domain contains two to three questions. Next to the question number is either a (T) or an (F). For example, under "Masking," question 5 on Figure 4-1, you'll find a (T). This means that if you answered it true, check the box. With question 13 on Figure 4-2, on the other hand, you'll find an (F). Only check that box if you answered the question false—and so on.

Your Style Under Stress score (Figure 4-1) will show you which forms of silence or violence you turn to most often. Your Dialogue Skills score (Figure 4-2) is organized by concept and chapter so you can decide which chapters may benefit you the most.

What Your Score Means

Your silence and violence scores give you a measure of how frequently you fall into these less-than-perfect strategies. It's actually possible to score high in both. A high score (one or two checked boxes per domain) means you use this technique fairly often. It also means you're human. Most people toggle between holding back and becoming too forceful.

The seven domains in Figure 4-2 reflect your skills in each of the corresponding seven skill chapters. If you score high (two or

Silence ☐	Violence ☐
Masking ☐ 5 (T) ☐ 6 (T)	**Controlling** ☐ 7 (T) ☐ 8 (T)
Avoiding ☐ 3 (T) ☐ 4 (T)	**Labeling** ☐ 9 (T) ☐ 10 (T)
Withdrawing ☐ 1 (T) ☐ 2 (T)	**Attacking** ☐ 11 (T) ☐ 12 (T)

Figure 4-1. Score Sheet for Style Under Stress Assessment

three boxes) in one of these domains, you're already quite skilled in this area. If you score low (zero or one), you may want to pay special attention to these chapters.

Since these scores represent how you typically *behave* during stressful or crucial conversations, they can change. Your score doesn't represent an inalterable character trait or a genetic propensity. It's merely a measure of your behavior—and you can change that. In fact, people who take this book seriously will practice the skills contained in each chapter and eventually they will change. And when they do, so will their lives.

What next? Now that you've identified your own Style Under Stress, you have a tool that can help you Learn to Look. That is, as you enter a touchy conversation, you can make a special effort

Ch 3: Start with Heart	Ch 7: STATE My Path
☐ 13 (F) ☐ ☐ 19 (F) ☐ 25 (F)	☐ 17 (T) ☐ ☐ 23 (F) ☐ 29 (T)
Ch 4: Learn to Look	Ch 8: Explore Others' Paths
☐ 14 (F) ☐ ☐ 20 (T) ☐ 26 (T)	☐ ☐ 18 (T) ☐ 24 (T) ☐ 30 (T)
Ch 5: Make It Safe	Ch 9: Move to Action
☐ 15 (T) ☐ ☐ 21 (T) ☐ 27 (F)	☐ 31 (F) ☐ ☐ 32 (F) ☐ 33 (F)
Ch 6: Master My Stories	
☐ ☐ 16 (T) ☐ 22 (F) ☐ 28 (F)	

Figure 4–2. Score Sheet for Dialogue Skills Assessment

to avoid some of your silence or violence habits. Also, when you're in the middle of a crucial conversation, you can be more conscious of what to watch for.

SUMMARY—LEARN TO LOOK

When caught up in a crucial conversation, it's difficult to see exactly what's going on and why. When a discussion starts to become stressful, we often end up doing the exact opposite of what works. We turn to the less healthy components of our Style Under Stress.

Learn to Look

To break from this insidious cycle, Learn to Look.

- Learn to look at content *and* conditions.
- Look for when things become crucial.
- Learn to watch for safety problems.
- Look to see if others are moving toward silence or violence.
- Look for outbreaks of your Style Under Stress.

5

Make It Safe

How to Make It Safe to Talk about Almost Anything

The last chapter contained a promise: If you spot safety risks as they happen, you can step out of the conversation, *build safety*, and then find a way to dialogue about almost anything. In this chapter we'll fulfill that promise by teaching what it takes to restore safety.

To get started, let's examine a situation where safety is at risk. We'll eavesdrop on a couple as they try to discuss one of the most delicate of topics— physical intimacy.

First a little background. Jotham thinks he and Yvonne are intimate with each other far too seldom. Yvonne is satisfied with their physical relationship. For years the two have acted out rather than talked out their concerns. When Jotham wants to be amorous and

Yvonne doesn't respond, he goes to silence. He pouts, says almost nothing, and avoids Yvonne for the next few days.

Yvonne knows what's going on with Jotham. Occasionally she'll go along with him even when she's not feeling particularly romantic. She does this in hopes of avoiding Jotham's pouting. Unfortunately, she then feels resentful toward Jotham, and it's much longer before she feels genuinely romantic toward him.

So here's the game. The more Jotham insists and pouts, the less attractive and interesting he is to Yvonne. The more Yvonne succumbs and then resents, the less she's interested in the entire relationship. The more both of them act out rather than talk out this crucial conversation, the more likely they are to end up going their separate ways. Yvonne has decided to broach the subject with Jotham. Rather than waiting until they're both upset, she's picked a time when they're relaxing on the couch. Here goes.

> YVONNE: Jotham, can we talk about what happened last night—you know, when I told you that I was tired?
>
> JOTHAM: I don't know if *I'm* in the mood.
>
> YVONNE: What's that supposed to mean?
>
> JOTHAM: I'm sick and tired of you deciding when we do what!
>
> YVONNE: (*walks out*)

STEP OUT. MAKE IT SAFE. THEN STEP BACK IN

Okay, let's look at Yvonne. She tried to tackle a tough topic. Good for her. She was already uncomfortable and her partner took a cheap shot at her. Some help he was. Now what should she do? How can she get back to honest and healthy dialogue? What do you do when you don't feel like it's safe to share what's on your mind?

The key is to step out of the content of the conversation. Don't stay stuck in what's being said. Yvonne exited because she was focused on *what* Jotham was saying. If she had been looking at Jotham's behavior, she would have spotted his use of sarcasm— a form of *masking*. Rather than talking out his concern, he's taking a potshot. Why would he do that? *Because he doesn't feel safe using dialogue.* But Yvonne missed this point.

Now, we're not suggesting that Jotham's behavior is acceptable, or that Yvonne should put up with it. But first things first—Start with Heart. The first question is: "What do I really want?"

If you really want to have a healthy conversation about a topic that will make or break your relationship, then for a moment or two you may have to set aside confronting the current issue— i.e., Jotham's sarcasm.

Yvonne's challenge here is to build safety—enough so that she can talk about their physical relationship, about the way Jotham is dealing with it, or about any other concerns. But if she doesn't make it safe, all she's going to get is a continuation of the silence and violence games.

So, what should she do?

In these circumstances, the *worst* at dialogue do what both Jotham and Yvonne did. Like Jotham, they totally ignore the crying need for more safety. They say whatever is on their minds— with no regard for how it will be received. Or like Yvonne, they conclude the topic is completely unsafe and move to silence.

The *good* realize that safety is at risk, but they fix it in exactly the wrong way. They try to make the subject more palatable by sugarcoating their message. "Oh, honey, I really want to be with you but I'm under a lot of pressure at work, and the stress makes it hard for me to enjoy our time together." They try to make things safer by watering down their content. This strategy, of course, avoids the real problem, and it never gets fixed.

The *best* don't play games. They know that dialogue is the free flow of meaning—with no pretending, sugarcoating, or faking. So they do something completely different. They step out of the content of the conversation, make it safe, and then step back in.

Once you've spotted safety problems, you can talk about the most challenging of topics by stepping out of the content and building enough safety that almost anything becomes discussable. For example: "Can we change gears for a minute? I'd like to talk about what happens when we're not romantically in sync. It would be good if we could both share what's working and what isn't. My goal isn't to make you feel guilty, and I certainly don't want to become defensive. What I'd really love is for us to come up with a solution that makes us both satisfied in our relationship."

NOTICE WHICH CONDITION IS AT RISK

Now, let's look at a couple of pieces that help us establish safety—even when the topic is high risk, controversial, and emotional. The first step to building more safety is to understand which of the two conditions of safety is at risk. Each requires a different solution.

Mutual Purpose

Why Talk in the First Place?

Remember the last time someone gave you difficult feedback and you didn't become defensive? Say a friend said some things to you that most people might get upset over. In order for this person to be able to deliver the delicate message, you must have believed he or she cared about you, or about your goals and objectives. That means you trusted his or her *purposes* so you were willing to listen to some pretty tough feedback.

Crucial conversations often go awry not because of the *content* of the conversation, but because others believe that the painful and pointed content means that you have a malicious *intent*. How can they feel safe when they believe you're out to do them harm? Soon, every word out of your mouth is suspect.

Consequently, the first condition of safety is *Mutual Purpose*. Mutual Purpose means that others perceive that we are working toward a common outcome in the conversation, that we care about their goals, interests, and values. And vice versa. We believe they care about ours. Consequently, Mutual Purpose is the entry condition of dialogue. Find a shared goal and you have both a good reason and a healthy climate for talking.

For example, if Jotham believes that Yvonne's purpose in raising this topic is to make him feel guilty or to get her way, this conversation is doomed from the outset. If he believes she really cares about making things better for him and herself, she may have a chance.

Watch for signs that Mutual Purpose is at risk. How do we know when the safety problem we're seeing is due to a lack of Mutual Purpose? It's actually fairly easy to spot. First and foremost, when purpose is at risk, we end up in debate. When others start forcing their opinions into the pool of meaning, it's often because they figure that we're trying to win and they need to do the same. Other signs that purpose is at risk include defensiveness, hidden agendas (the silence form of fouled-up purpose), accusations, and circling back to the same topic. Here are some crucial questions to help us determine when Mutual Purpose is at risk:

- Do others believe I care about their goals in this conversation?
- Do they trust my motives?

Remember the Mutual *in Mutual Purpose.* Just a word to the wise. Mutual Purpose is not a technique. To succeed in crucial conversations, we must really care about the interests of others— not just our own. The purpose has to be truly mutual. If our goal is to get our way or manipulate others, it will quickly become apparent, safety will be destroyed, and we'll be back to silence and violence in no time. Before you begin, examine your motives. Ask yourself the Start with Heart questions:

- What do I want for me?

- What do I want for others?

- What do I want for the relationship?

Look for the mutuality. Let's see how Mutual Purpose applies to a tough example—one where, at first glance, it might appear as if your purpose is to make things better for yourself. How can you find Mutual Purpose in this? Let's say you've got a boss who frequently fails to keep commitments. How could you tell the boss you don't trust him? Surely there's no way to say this without the boss becoming defensive or vengeful, because he knows that your goal is merely to make your life better.

To avoid disaster, find a Mutual Purpose that would be so motivating to the boss that he'd want to hear your concerns. If your only reason for approaching the boss is to get what you want, the boss will hear you as critical and selfish—which is what you are. On the other hand, if you try to see the other person's point of view, you can often find a way to draw the other person willingly into even very sensitive conversations. For example, if the boss's behavior is causing you to miss deadlines he cares about, or incur costs he frets over, or lose productivity that he worries about, then you're onto a possible Mutual Purpose.

Imagine raising the topic this way: "I've got some ideas for how I can be much more reliable and even reduce costs by a few thousand dollars in preparing the report each month. It's going to be a bit of a sensitive conversation—but I think it will help a great deal if we can talk about it."

Mutual Respect

Will We Be Able to Remain in Dialogue?

While it's true that there's no reason to enter a crucial conversation if you don't have Mutual Purpose, it's equally true that you can't stay in the conversation if you don't maintain Mutual Respect. Mutual Respect is the continuance condition of dialogue. As people perceive that others don't respect them, the conversation immediately becomes unsafe and dialogue comes to a screeching halt.

Why? Because respect is like air. If you take it away, it's all people can think about. The instant people perceive disrespect in a conversation, the interaction is no longer about the original purpose—it is now about defending dignity.

For example, you're talking with a group of supervisors about a complicated quality problem. You really want to see the problem resolved once and for all. Your job depends on it. Unfortunately, you also think the supervisors are overpaid and underqualified. You firmly believe that not only are they in over their heads, but they do stupid things all the time. Some of them even act unethically.

As the supervisors throw out ideas, you roll your eyes. The disrespect you carry in your head creeps out in one unfortunate gesture. And it's all over. What happens to the conversation despite the fact that you still share a common objective? It tanks. They take shots at your proposals. You add insulting adjectives in describing theirs. As attention turns to scoring points, everyone loses. Your Mutual Purpose suffers for a lack of Mutual Respect.

Telltale signs. To spot when respect is violated and safety takes a turn south, watch for signs that people are defending their dignity. Emotions are the key. When people feel disrespected, they become highly charged. Their emotions turn from fear to anger.

Then they resort to pouting, name-calling, yelling, and making threats. Ask the following question to determine when Mutual Respect is at risk:

- Do others believe I respect them?

Can You Respect People You Don't Respect?

Some people fear they'll never be able to maintain Mutual Purpose or Mutual Respect with certain individuals or in certain circumstances. How, they wonder, can they share the same purpose with people who come from completely different backgrounds or whose morals or values differ from theirs? What do you do, for example, if you're upset because another person has let you down? And if this has repeatedly happened, how can you respect a person who is so poorly motivated and selfish?

Yvonne is struggling with this exact point. There are times when she doesn't even *like* Jotham. She sees him as whiny and self-centered. How can you speak respectfully with someone like *that*?

Dialogue truly would be doomed if we had to share every objective or respect every element of another person's character before we could talk. If this were the case, we'd all be mute. We can, however, stay in dialogue by finding a way to honor and regard another person's basic humanity. In essence, feelings of disrespect often come when we dwell on how others are *different* from ourselves. We can counteract these feelings by looking for ways we are similar. Without excusing their behavior, we try to sympathize, even empathize, with them.

A rather clever person once hinted how to do this in the form of a prayer—"Lord, help me forgive those who sin *differently* than I." When we recognize that we all have weaknesses, it's easier to find a way to respect others. When we do this, we feel a kinship, a sense of mutuality between ourselves and even the thorniest of people. It is this sense of kinship and connection to others that motivates us to enter tough conversations, and it eventually enables us to stay in dialogue with virtually anyone.

Consider the following example. A manufacturing company has been out on strike for over six months. Finally, the union agrees to return to work, but the represented employees have to sign a contract that is actually worse than what they were originally demanding. The first day back it's clear that although people will work, they won't do so with a smile and a spring in their step. Everyone is furious. How are people ever going to move ahead?

Concerned that although the strike is over, the battle isn't, a manager asks one of the authors to lend a hand. So he meets with the two groups of leaders (both managers and union heads) and asks them to do one thing. Each group is to go into a separate room and write out its goals for the company on flip-chart-sized paper. For two hours each group feverishly lays out what it wants in the future and then tapes the lists to the wall. When they finish their assignment, the groups then swap places with the goal of finding anything—maybe just a morsel—but anything they might have in common.

After a few minutes the two groups return to the training room. They're positively stunned. It was as if they had written the exact same lists. They didn't merely share the shadow of an idea or two. Their aspirations were nearly identical. All wanted a profitable company, stable and rewarding jobs, high-quality products, and a positive impact on the community. Given a chance to speak freely and without fear of attack, each group laid out not simply what *it* wanted, but what virtually every person wanted.

This experience caused each group to seriously question how it had seen the other side. The groups began to see others as more similar to themselves. They realized the petty and political tactics the others had used were embarrassingly similar to the ones they themselves had employed. The "sins" of others were different from their own more because of the role they played than because of a fundamental blight on their character. They restored Mutual Respect, and dialogue replaced silence and violence for the first time in decades.

WHAT TO DO ONCE YOU STEP OUT

When you see that either Mutual Respect or Purpose is at risk, we've suggested that you shouldn't ignore it. We've also argued that you should be able to find a way to both find Mutual Purpose and enjoy Mutual Respect—even with people who are enormously different.

But how? What are you supposed to actually do? We've shared a few modest ideas (mostly things to avoid), so let's get into three hard-hitting skills that the best at dialogue use:

- Apologize

- Contrast

- CRIB

Each skill helps rebuild either Mutual Respect or Mutual Purpose. First, we'll study them in action. Then, we'll see if they might help Yvonne get things back on track.

Where were you? You're talking with a group of hourly employees who worked all night preparing for a factory tour. You were supposed to bring the division vice president by, and the team members were then going to update him on a new process they've put into place. They're proud of some improvements they've recently made—enough so that they willingly worked straight through the night to finish the last details.

Unfortunately, when it came time to swing by their area, the visiting VP dropped a bomb. He laid out a plan you're convinced would hurt quality and potentially drive away your biggest customers. Since you only had another hour with the VP, you chose to talk through the issue rather than conduct the tour. Your future depended on that particular conversation. Fortunately, you were able to avert the plan. Unfortunately, you forgot to get word to the team that had worked so hard.

As you walked back to your office after escorting the executive to his car, you bumped into the team. Bleary-eyed and disappointed, all six of them were now fuming. No visit, no phone call, and now it was clear from the way you were sprinting on by that you weren't even going to stop and give them a simple explanation.

Ouch.

That's when things started turning ugly. "We pulled an all-nighter, and you didn't even bother to come by! That's the last time we're busting our hump for you!"

Time stands still. This conversation has just turned crucial. The employees who had worked so hard are obviously upset. They feel disrespected.

But you miss that point. Why? Because now *you* feel disrespected. They've attacked you. So you stay stuck in the content of the conversation—thinking this has something to do with the factory tour.

> "I had to choose between the future of the company and the plant tour. I chose our future, and I'd do it again if I had to."

Now both you and they are fighting for respect. This is getting you nowhere fast. But what else could you do?

Instead of getting hooked and fighting back, break the cycle. See their aggressive behavior for what it is—a sign of violated safety—then step out of the conversation, build safety, and step back into the content. Here's how.

Apologize When Appropriate

When you've made a mistake that has hurt others (e.g., you didn't call the team), start with an apology. An apology is a statement that sincerely expresses your sorrow for your role in causing—or at least not preventing—pain or difficulty to others.

> "I'm sorry I didn't give you a call when I learned that we wouldn't be coming by. You worked all night, it would have been a wonderful chance to showcase your improvements, and I didn't even explain what happened. I apologize."

Now, an apology isn't really an apology unless you experience a change in heart. To offer a sincere apology, your motives have to change. You have to give up saving face, being right, or winning in order to focus on what you *really* want. You have to sacrifice a bit of your ego by admitting your error. But like many sacrifices, when you give up something you value, you're rewarded with something even more valuable—healthy dialogue and better results. Then watch to see if this sincere show of respect has helped restore safety. If it has, you can now explain the details of what happened. If it hasn't, you'll need to use one of the more advanced skills that follow in the next few pages. In any case, first make it safe; then return to the issue.

When your behavior has given someone clear cause to doubt your respect or commitment to Mutual Purpose, your conversation will end up in silly game-playing and frustrating misunderstandings until you offer a sincere apology.

Contrast to Fix Misunderstanding

Sometimes others feel disrespected during crucial conversations even though we haven't done anything disrespectful. Sure, there are times when respect gets violated because we behave in clearly hurtful ways. But just as often, the insult is entirely unintended.

The same can happen with Mutual Purpose. You can start by innocently sharing your views, but the other person believes your intention is to beat him or her up or coerce him or her into accepting your opinion. Clearly an apology is not appropriate in these circumstances. It would be disingenuous to admit you were wrong when you weren't. How, then, can you rebuild Mutual Purpose or Mutual Respect in order to make it safe to get back to dialogue?

When others misinterpret either your purpose or your intent, step out of the argument and rebuild safety by using a skill called *Contrasting.*

Contrasting is a don't/do statement that:

- Addresses others' concerns that you don't respect them or that you have a malicious purpose (the *don't* part).

- Confirms your respect or clarifies your real purpose (the *do* part).

For example:

> [The *don't* part] "The last thing I wanted to do was communicate that I don't value the work you put in or that I didn't want to share it with the VP.
> [The *do* part] I think your work has been nothing short of spectacular."

Now that you've addressed the threat to safety, you can return to the issue of the visit itself and move to remediation:

> "Unfortunately, just when I was starting to make the trip out here, an issue came up with the VP that I needed to address right then and there, or it could have cost us a huge piece of our business. I tell you what—I'll see if I can get him down here sometime tomorrow to review your work. He'll be here for the ribbon-cutting ceremony. Let's see if we can show off the process improvements you came up with."

Of the two parts of Contrasting, the *don't* is the more important because it deals with the misunderstanding that has put safety at risk. The employees who worked so hard are acting on the belief that you don't appreciate their efforts and didn't care enough to keep them informed—when the opposite was true. So you address the misunderstanding by explaining what you don't intend. Once you've done this, and safety returns to the conversation, then you can explain what you do intend. Safety first.

Let's go back to Yvonne and Jotham. Yvonne is trying to get the conversation going, and Jotham suspects her motives. Let's see how Contrasting might help her.

> YVONNE: I think it makes things worse when you withdraw and won't talk to me for days at a time.

> JOTHAM: So you expect me not only to put up with regular rejection, but also to be sociable and happy when I do?

Jotham appears to believe that Yvonne's motive is to reshape him. It's unsafe. Mutual Purpose is at risk. Rather than responding to his sarcasm, she should step out of the content and clarify her real motives.

> YVONNE: I don't want to suggest that this problem is yours. The truth is, I think it's ours. I'm not trying to put the burden on you. I don't even know what the solution is. What I do want is to be able to talk so that we can understand each other better. Perhaps that will help me change how I'm responding to you, too.

> JOTHAM: I know where this is going. We talk, I continue to get rejected, but you get to feel good about yourself because "we've communicated." Have you been watching *Oprah* again?

Obviously Jotham still believes that Yvonne merely wants to confirm that their existing relationship is okay and if she does, she'll be able to continue to reject Jotham—but feel good about it. Jotham still feels unsafe. So Yvonne continues to step out and build safety, using Contrasting.

> YVONNE: Seriously, Honey. I'm not interested in discussing why our current relationship is really okay. I can see that it isn't. I merely want to talk about what each of us likes and doesn't like. That way we'll be able to see what we need to improve and why. My only goal is to come up with some ideas that will make both of us happy.

> JOTHAM: (*Changing tone and demeanor*) Really? I'm sorry to be so insecure about this. I know I'm being a bit selfish about things, but I don't know how to make myself feel differently.

Contrasting is not apologizing. It's important to understand that Contrasting is *not* apologizing. It is not a way of taking back something we've said that hurt others' feelings. Rather, it is a way of ensuring what we said didn't hurt more than it should have. Once Yvonne clarified her genuine goals (and not merely some trumped-up goal that appeals to Jotham), Jotham felt safer acknowledging his own contribution, and the two were back in dialogue.

Contrasting provides context and proportion. When we're in the middle of a touchy conversation, sometimes others hear what we're saying as bigger or worse than we intend. For example, you talk with your assistant about his lack of punctuality. When you share your concern, he appears crushed.

At this point you could be tempted to water down your content—"You know it's really not that big a deal." Don't do it. Don't take back what you've said. Instead, put it in context. For instance, at this point your assistant may believe you are completely dissatisfied with his performance. He believes that your view of the issue at hand represents the totality of your respect for him. If this belief is incorrect, use Contrasting to clarify what you don't and do believe. Start with what you don't believe.

> "Let me put this in perspective. I don't want you to think I'm not satisfied with the quality of your work. I want us to continue working together. I really do think you're doing a good job. This punctuality issue is important to me, and I'd just like you to work on that. If you will be more attentive to that, there are no other issues."

Use Contrasting for prevention or first aid. Contrasting is useful both as a prevention and as first aid for safety problems. So far our examples have been of the first-aid type. Someone has taken something wrong, and we've intervened to clarify our true purpose or meaning.

When we're aware that something we're *about* to drop into the pool of meaning could create a splash of defensiveness, we use Contrasting to bolster safety—even before we see others going to either silence or violence.

> "I don't want you to think that I don't appreciate the time you've taken to keep our checkbook balanced and up to date. I do appreciate it, and I know I certainly couldn't have done nearly as well. I do, however, have some concerns with how we're using the new electronic banking system."

When people misunderstand and you start arguing over the misunderstanding, stop. Use Contrasting. Explain what you don't mean until you've restored safety. Then return to the conversation. Safety first.

You Try

Let's practice. Read the situations below and then come up with your own Contrasting statements. Remember, contrast what you don't want or intend with what you actually do want or intend. Say it in a way that helps make it safe for the other person.

Angry roommate. You asked your roommate to move her things in the refrigerator off your shelves and onto her shelves. You thought it was no big deal, simply a request to share the space evenly. You have no hidden agenda. You like this roommate a great deal. She came back with: "There you go again, telling me how to run my life. I can't change the vacuum cleaner bag without you jumping in and giving me advice."

Formulate a Contrasting statement.

I don't want _____

I do want _____

Touchy employee. You're about to talk to Jacob, an employee who continually blows up when people try to give him feedback. Yesterday a coworker told Jacob that she'd prefer it if he would clean up after himself in the lunchroom (something that everyone else does), and Jacob blew up. You've decided to say something. Of course, you'll be giving him feedback, and that's what usually sets him off, so you'll need to be careful up front. You'll want to set the right tone and lay out the context carefully. After all, you like Jacob a lot. Everyone does. He has a great sense of humor and is the most competent and hard-working employee around. If he could only be less touchy.

Formulate a Contrasting statement.

I don't want _____

I do want _____

Chatty teenager. Your teenage nephew moved in with you when his father (your brother) passed away and your sister-in-law could no longer handle him. He was starting to hang with the wrong crowd. He has always gotten along with you, and things have been going well except in one area: He spends hours on the phone and Internet—most of his waking hours. In light of what he could be doing, you're not really disturbed, but it has been hard for you to make calls and check your email. You said something to him about cutting back his time on the phone and online, and he came back with: "Please don't send me to a youth home! I'll be good! I promise. I'll stop talking to my friends; just don't send me away."

Formulate a contrasting statement.

I don't want_____

I do want_____

CRIB TO GET TO MUTUAL PURPOSE

Let's add one more skill. Sometimes we find ourselves in the middle of a debate because we clearly have different purposes. There is no misunderstanding here. Contrasting won't do the trick. We need something sturdier for this job.

For instance, you've just been offered a promotion that will help propel your career along a faster track and bring you a great deal more authority, and it pays enough to help soften the blow of displacement. That last part is important because you'll have to move the family across the country and your spouse and kids love where you currently live.

You expected your spouse to have feelings of ambivalence over the move, but he or she doesn't seem to be bivaling even a tiny bit. To your spouse the promotion is a bad news/bad news event. First, you have to move, and second, you'll work even longer hours. That whole thing about more money and power doesn't seem to be compensating. Now what?

The *worst* at dialogue either ignore the problem and push ahead or roll over and let others have their way. They opt for either competition or submission. Both strategies end up making winners and losers, and the problem continues long beyond the initial conversation.

The *good* at dialogue move immediately toward compromise. For example, the couple facing the transfer sets up two households—one where one spouse will be working and one where the family currently lives. Nobody really wants this arrangement, and frankly, it's a pretty ugly solution that's bound to lead to more serious problems, even divorce. While compromise is sometimes necessary, the best know better than to start there.

The *best* at dialogue use four skills to look for a Mutual Purpose. The four skills they use form the acronym CRIB.

Commit to Seek Mutual Purpose

As is true with most dialogue skills, if you want to get back to dialogue, you have to Start with Heart. In this case, you have to *agree to agree*. To be successful, we have to stop using silence or violence to compel others to our view. We must even surrender false dialogue, where we pretend to have Mutual Purpose (calmly arguing our side until the other person gives in). We Start with Heart by committing to stay in the conversation until we come up with a solution that serves a purpose we both share.

This can be tough. To stop arguing, we have to suspend our belief that our choice is the absolute best and only one, and that we'll never be happy until we get exactly what we currently want. We have to open our mind to the fact that maybe, just maybe, there is a different choice out there—one that suits everyone.

We also have to be willing to verbalize this commitment even when our partner seems committed to winning. We act on faith that our partner is stuck in silence or violence because he or she feels unsafe. We assume that if we build more safety—by demonstrating our commitment to finding a Mutual Purpose—the other person will feel more confident that dialogue could be a productive avenue.

So next time you find yourself stuck in a battle of wills, try this amazingly powerful but simple skill. Step out of the content of the struggle and make it safe. Simply say, "It seems like we're both trying to force our view. I commit to stay in this discussion until we have a solution both of us are happy with." Then watch whether safety takes a turn for the better.

Recognize the Purpose behind the Strategy

Wanting to come up with a shared goal is a wonderful first step, but it's not enough. Once we've had a change of heart, we need to change our strategy. Here's the problem we have to fix: When we find ourselves at an impasse, it's because we're asking for one thing and the other person is asking for something else. We think we'll never find a way out because we equate what we're asking for with what we want. In truth, what we're asking for is the *strategy* we're suggesting to get what we want. We confuse wants or purpose with strategies. That's the problem.

For example, I come home from work and say that I want to go to a movie. You say that you want to stay home and relax. And so we debate: movie, TV, movie, read, etc. We figure we'll never be able to resolve our differences because going out and staying home are incompatible.

In such circumstances we can break the impasse by asking others, "Why do you want that?" In this case,

"Why do you want to stay home?"

"Because I'm tired of running around and dealing with the hassle of the city."

"So you want peace and quiet?"

"Mostly. And why do you want to go to a movie?"

"So I can spend some time with you away from the kids."

Before you can agree on a Mutual Purpose, you must know what people's real purposes are. So step out of the content of the conversation—which is generally focused on strategies—and explore the purposes behind them.

When you do this, new options become possible. When you release your grip on your strategy and focus on your real purpose, you open up the possibility of finding new alternatives that can serve Mutual Purpose.

"You want peace and quiet, and I want time with you away from the kids. So if we can come up with something that is quiet and away, we'll both be happy. Is that right?"

"Absolutely. What if we were to take a drive up the canyon and . . ."

Invent a Mutual Purpose

Sometimes when we recognize the purposes behind our strategies, we discover that we actually have compatible goals. From there you simply come up with common strategies. But we're not always so lucky. For example, you find out that your genuine wants and goals cannot be served except at the expense of the other person's. In this case you cannot *discover* a Mutual Purpose, so you must actively *invent* one.

To invent a Mutual Purpose, move to more encompassing goals. Find an objective that is more meaningful or more rewarding than the ones that divide the various sides. For instance, you and your spouse may not agree on whether or not you should take the promotion, but you can agree that the needs of your relationship and the children come before career aspirations. By focusing on higher and longer-term goals, you can find a way to transcend short-term compromises, build Mutual Purpose, and get to dialogue.

Brainstorm New Strategies

Once you've built safety by finding a shared purpose, you should now have enough safety to return to the content of the conversation. It's time to step back into the dialogue and brainstorm strategies that meet everyone's needs. If you've committed to finding something everyone can agree on, and surfaced what you really want, you'll no longer be spending your energy on unproductive conflict. Instead, you'll be actively coming up with options that can serve everyone.

Suspend judgment and think outside the box for new alternatives. Can you find a way to work in a job that is local and still meets your career goals? Is *this* job with *this* company the only thing that will make you happy? Is a move really necessary in this new job? Is there another community that could offer your family the same benefits? If you're not willing to give creativity a try, it'll be impossible for you to jointly come up with a mutually acceptable option. If you are, the sky's the limit.

CRIB to Get to Mutual Purpose

So when you sense that you and others are working at cross-purposes, here's what you can do. First, step out of the content of the conflict. Stop focusing on who thinks what. Then CRIB your way to Mutual Purpose.

- *Commit to seek Mutual Purpose.* Make a unilateral public commitment to stay in the conversation until you come up with something that serves everyone.

  "This isn't working. Your team is arguing to stay late and work until we're done, and my team wants to go home and come back on the weekend. Why don't we see if we can come up with something that satisfies everyone?"

- *Recognize the purpose behind the strategy.* Ask people why they want what they're pushing for. Separate what they're demanding from the purpose it serves.

  "Exactly why don't you want to come in Saturday morning? We're feeling fatigued and are worried about safety issues and a loss of quality. Why do you want to stay late?"

- *Invent a Mutual Purpose.* If after clarifying everyone's purposes you are still at odds, see if you can invent a higher or longer-term purpose that is more motivating than the ones that keep you in conflict.

  "I certainly don't want to make winners and losers here. It's far better if we can come up with something that doesn't make one team resent the other one. We've voted before or flipped a coin, and the losers just ended up resenting the winners. I'm more worried about how we feel about each other than anything else. Let's make sure that whatever we do, we don't drive a wedge in our working relationship."

- *Brainstorm new strategies.* With a clear Mutual Purpose, you can join forces in searching for a solution that serves everyone.

  "So we need to come up with something that doesn't jeopardize safety and quality and allows your team to attend their colleague's wedding on Saturday. My team members don't care about the game a bit. What if we were to work the morning and

early afternoon, and then you come in after the game and take over from there? That way we'll be able . . ."

BACK TO YVONNE AND JOTHAM

Let's end where we started. Yvonne is going to try to move to dialogue with Jotham. Let's see how she does at making it safe in her crucial conversation. First, she'll use Contrasting to prevent misunderstanding of her purpose.

> YVONNE: Jotham, I'd like to talk about our physical relation-ship. I'm not doing it to put you on the spot or to suggest the problem is yours. I'm completely clear that it's as much my problem as yours. I'd really like to talk about it so we can make things better for both of us.
>
> JOTHAM: What's there to talk about? You don't want it. I want it. I'll try to deal with it.
>
> YVONNE: I think it's more complicated than that. The way you act sometimes makes me want to be with you even less.
>
> JOTHAM: If that's how you feel, why are we pretending we have a relationship at all?

Okay, what just happened? Remember, we're exploring Yvonne's side of the conversation. She's the one initiating the talk. Clearly there's a lot Jotham could be doing to make things go better. But she's not Jotham. What should Yvonne do? She should focus on what she really wants: to find a way to make things better for both of them. Consequently, she shouldn't respond to the content of Jotham's discouraging statement. Rather, she should look at the safety issue behind it. Why is Jotham starting to withdraw from the conversation? Two reasons:

- The way Yvonne made her point sounded to him like she was blaming him for everything.

- He believes her concern in one small area reflects her total feelings toward him.

So she'll apologize and use Contrasting to rebuild safety.

YVONNE: I'm sorry I said it that way. I'm not blaming you for how I feel or act. That's my problem. I don't see this as your problem. I see it as our problem. Both of us may be acting in ways that make things worse. I know I am at least.

JOTHAM: I probably am too. Sometimes I pout because I'm hurting. And I also do it hoping it'll make you feel bad. I'm sorry about that, too.

Notice what just happened. Since Yvonne dealt well with the safety issue and kept focused on what she really wanted out of this conversation, Jotham returned to the conversation. This is far more effective than if Yvonne had gone into blaming.

Let's continue.

JOTHAM: I just don't see how we can work this out. I'm wired for more passion than you are—it seems like the only solution is for me to put up with it the way it is or for you to feel like a sex slave.

The problem now is one of Mutual Purpose. Jotham thinks he and Yvonne are at cross-purposes. In his mind, there is no possibility of a mutually satisfactory solution. Rather than move to compromise or fight for her way, Yvonne will step out of the issue and CRIB to get to Mutual Purpose.

YVONNE: [*Commit to seek Mutual Purpose*] No, that isn't what I want at all. I don't want anything with you that isn't great for both of us. I just want to find a way to have us both feel close, appreciated, and loved.

JOTHAM: That's what I want, too. It just seems like we get those feelings in different ways.

(Notice how Jotham is leaving the game behind and joining the dialogue. Safety—specifically Mutual Purpose—is making this possible.)

YVONNE: [*Recognize the purpose behind the strategy*] Maybe not. What makes you feel loved and appreciated?

JOTHAM: Making love with you when you really want to makes me feel loved and appreciated. And you?

YVONNE: When you do thoughtful things for me. And, I guess, when you hold me—but not always sexually.

JOTHAM: You mean, if we're just cuddling that makes you feel loved?

YVONNE: Yes. And sometimes—I guess when I think you're doing it because you love me—sex does that for me, too.

JOTHAM: [*Invent a Mutual Purpose*] So we need to find ways to be together that make both of us feel loved and appreciated. Is that what we're looking for here?

YVONNE: Yes. I really want that, too.

JOTHAM: [*Brainstorm new strategies*] Well, what if we . . .

BUT I COULD <u>NEVER</u> DO THAT!

Reading a complicated interaction like this one might lead to two reactions. First, you might think, "Wow, these ideas could actually work!" And at the same time, you could be thinking, "But there's no way I could think that clearly in the middle of that kind of delicate conversation!"

We admit that it's pretty easy for us to put all the skills together when we're sitting at a computer typing a script. But the good news is, that's not where these examples came from. They came from real experiences. People do act like this all the time. In fact, *you* do on your best days.

So don't overwhelm yourself by asking whether you could think this clearly during every heated and emotional conversation. Merely consider whether you could think a little more clearly during a few crucial conversations. Or prepare in advance. *Before* a crucial conversation begins, think about which skills will help you most. Remember, when it comes to these high-stakes conversations, a little progress can produce a lot of benefit.

Finally, as is the case with most complicated problems, don't aim for perfection. Aim for progress. Learn to slow the process down when your adrenaline gets pumping. Carry a few of the questions we're suggesting with you as you go. Pick the ones that you think are most relevant to the topic at hand. And watch yourself get better a little at a time.

SUMMARY—MAKE IT SAFE
Step Out

When others move to silence or violence, step out of the conversation and Make It Safe. When safety is restored, go back to the issue at hand and continue the dialogue.

Decide Which Condition of Safety Is at Risk

- *Mutual Purpose.* Do others believe you care about their goals in this conversation? Do they trust your motives?

- *Mutual Respect.* Do others believe you respect them?

Apologize When Appropriate

• When you've clearly violated respect, apologize.

Contrast to Fix Misunderstanding

• When others misunderstand either your purpose or your intent, use Contrasting. Start with what you *don't* intend or mean. Then explain what you *do* intend or mean.

CRIB to Get to Mutual Purpose

• When you are at cross-purposes, use four skills to get back to Mutual Purpose:

   • *C*ommit to seek Mutual Purpose.

   • *R*ecognize the purpose behind the strategy.

   • *I*nvent a Mutual Purpose.

   • *B*rainstorm new strategies.

6

*It's not how you play the game,
it's how the game plays you.*

Master My Stories

How to Stay in Dialogue When You're Angry, Scared, or Hurt

At this point you may be saying to yourself, "How am I supposed to remember to do all this stuff—especially when my emotions are raging like hot magma?"

This chapter explores how to gain control of crucial conversations by learning how to take charge of your emotions. By learning to exert influence over your own feelings, you'll place yourself in a far better position to use all the tools we've explored thus far.

HE MADE ME MAD!

How many times have you heard someone say: "He made me mad!"? How many times have you said it? For instance, you're sitting quietly at home watching TV and your mother-in-law (who lives with you) walks in. She glances around and then starts picking up the mess you made a few minutes earlier when you whipped up a batch of nachos. This ticks you off. She's always smugly skulking around the house, thinking you're a slob.

A few minutes later when your spouse asks you why you're so upset, you explain, "It's your mom again. I was lying here enjoying myself when she gave me that look, and it really got me going. To be honest, I wish she would quit doing that. It's my only day off, I'm relaxing quietly, and then she walks in and pushes my buttons."

"Does she push your buttons?" your spouse asks. "Or do you?"

That's an interesting question.

One thing's for certain. No matter who is doing the button pushing, some people tend to react more explosively than others—and to the same stimulus, no less. Why is that? For instance, what enables some people to listen to withering feedback without flinching, whereas others pitch a fit when you tell them they've got a smear of salsa on their chin? Why is it that sometimes you yourself can take a verbal blow to the gut without batting an eye, but other times you go ballistic if someone so much as looks at you sideways?

EMOTIONS DON'T JUST HAPPEN

To answer these questions, we'll start with two rather bold (and sometimes unpopular) claims. Then, having tipped our hand, we'll explain the logic behind each claim.

Claim One. Emotions don't settle upon you like a fog. They are not foisted upon you by others. No matter how comfortable it might make you feel saying it—others don't *make you mad*. You make you mad. You and only you create your emotions.

Claim Two. Once you've created your emotions, you have only two options: You can act on them or be acted on by them. That is, when it comes to strong emotions, you either find a way to master them or fall hostage to them.

Here's how this all unfolds.

MARIA'S STORY

Consider Maria, a copywriter who is currently hostage to some pretty strong emotions. She and her colleague Louis just reviewed the latest draft of a proposal with their boss. During the meeting, they were supposed to be jointly presenting their latest ideas. But when Maria paused to take a breath, Louis took over the presentation, making almost all the points they had come up with together. When the boss turned to Maria for input, there was nothing left for her to say.

Maria has been feeling humiliated and angry throughout this project. First, Louis took their suggestions to the boss and discussed them behind her back. Second, he completely monopolized the presentation. Consequently, Maria believes that Louis is downplaying her contribution because she's the only woman on the team.

She's getting fed up with his "boys' club" mentality. So what does she do? She doesn't want to appear "oversensitive," so most of the time she says nothing and just does her job. However, she does manage to assert herself by occasionally getting in sarcastic jabs about the way she's being treated.

"Sure I can get that printout for you. Should I just get your coffee and whip up a bundt cake while I'm at it?" she mutters, and rolls her eyes as she exits the room.

Louis, in turn, finds Maria's cheap shots and sarcasm puzzling. He's not sure what has Maria upset but is beginning to despise her smug attitude and hostile reaction to most everything he does. As a result, when the two work together, you could cut the tension with a knife.

What's Making Maria Mad?

The *worst* at dialogue fall into the trap Maria has fallen into. Maria is completely unaware of a dangerous assumption she's making. She's upset at being overlooked and is keeping a professional silence. She's assuming that her emotions and behavior are the only right and reasonable reactions under the circumstances. She's convinced that anyone in her place would feel the same way.

Here's the problem. Maria is treating her emotions as if they are the only valid response. Since, in her mind, they are both justified and accurate, she makes no effort to change or even question them. In fact, in her view, Louis caused them. Ultimately, her actions (saying nothing and taking cheap shots) are being driven by these very emotions. Since she's not acting *on* her emotions, her emotions are acting on her—controlling her behavior and driving her deteriorating relationship with Louis. The *worst* at dialogue are hostages to their emotions, and they don't even know it.

The *good* at dialogue realize that if they don't control their emotions, matters will get worse. So they try something else. They fake it. They choke down reactions and then do their best to get back to dialogue. At least, they give it a shot.

Unfortunately, once they hit a rough spot in a crucial conversation, their suppressed emotions come out of hiding. They show up as tightened jaws or sarcastic comments. Dialogue takes a hit. Or maybe their paralyzing fear causes them to avoid saying what they really think. Meaning is cut off at the source. In any case, their emotions sneak out of the cubbyhole they've been crammed into and find a way into the conversation. It's never pretty, and it always kills dialogue.

The *best* at dialogue do something completely different. They aren't held hostage by their emotions, nor do they try to hide or suppress them. Instead, they act *on* their emotions. That is, when they have strong feelings, they influence (and often change) their emotions by *thinking them out*. As a result, they choose their emotions, and by so doing, make it possible to choose behaviors that create better results.

This, of course, is easier said than done. How do you *rethink* yourself from an emotional and dangerous state into one that puts you back in control?

Where should Maria start? To help rethink or gain control of our emotions, let's see where our feelings come from in the first place. Let's look at a model that helps us first examine and then gain control of our own emotions.

Consider Maria. She's feeling hurt but is worried that if she says something to Louis, she'll look too emotional, so she alternates between holding her feelings inside (avoiding) and taking cheap shots (masking).

As Figure 6-1 demonstrates, Maria's actions stem from her feelings. First she feels and then she acts. That's easy enough, but it

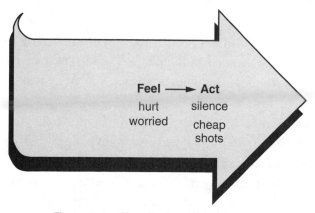

Figure 6-1. How Feelings Drive Actions

begs the question: What's causing Maria's feelings in the first place?

Is it Louis's behavior? As was the case with the nacho-mother-in-law, did Louis *make* Maria feel insulted and hurt? Maria heard and saw Louis do something, she generated an emotion, and then she acted out her feelings—using forms of masking and avoiding.

So here's the big question: What happens between Louis acting and Maria feeling? Is there an intermediate step that turns someone else's actions into our feelings? If not, then it has to be true that others make us feel the way we do.

Stories Create Feelings

As it turns out, there *is* an intermediate step between what others do and how we feel. That's why, when faced with the same circumstances, ten people may have ten different emotional responses. For instance, with a coworker like Louis, some might feel insulted whereas others merely feel curious. Some become angry and others feel concern or even sympathy.

What is this intermediate step? Just *after* we observe what others do and just *before* we feel some emotion about it, we tell ourselves a story. That is, we add meaning to the action we observed. To the simple behavior we add motive. Why were they doing that? We also add judgment—is that good or bad? And then, based on these thoughts or stories, our body responds with an emotion.

Pictorially it looks like the model in Figure 6-2. We call this model our Path to Action because it explains how emotions, thoughts, and experiences lead to our actions.

You'll note that we've added telling a story to our model. We observe, *we tell a story*, and then we feel. Although this addition complicates things a bit, it also gives us hope. Since we *and only*

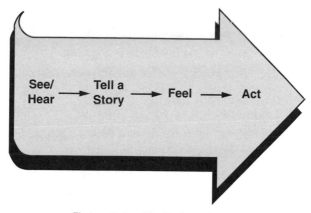

Figure 6-2.   The Path to Action

we are telling the story, we can take back control of our own emotions by telling a different story. We now have a point of leverage or control. If we can find a way to control the stories we tell, by rethinking or retelling them, we can master our emotions and, therefore, master our crucial conversations.

OUR STORIES

> *"Nothing in this world is good or bad,*
> *but thinking makes it so."*
> —WILLIAM SHAKESPEARE

Stories explain what's going on. Exactly what are our stories? They are our interpretations of the facts. They help explain what we see and hear. They're theories we use to explain *why, how,* and *what.* For instance, Maria asks: "Why does Louis take over? He doesn't trust my ability to communicate. He thinks that because I'm a woman, people won't listen to me."

Our stories also help explain how. "How am I supposed to judge all of this? Is this a good or a bad thing? Louis thinks I'm incompetent, and this is bad."

Finally, a story might also include what. "What should I do about all this? If I say something, he'll think I'm a whiner or oversensitive or militant, so it's best to clam up."

Of course, as we come up with our own meaning or stories, it isn't long until our body responds with strong feelings or emotions—they're directly linked to our judgments of right/wrong, good/bad, kind/selfish, fair/unfair, etc. Maria's story yields anger and frustration. These feelings, in turn, drive Maria to her actions—toggling back and forth between clamming up and taking an occasional cheap shot (see Figure 6-3).

Even if you don't realize it, you are telling yourself stories. When we teach people that it's our stories that drive our emotions and not other people's actions, someone inevitably raises a hand and says, "Wait a minute! I didn't notice myself telling a story. When that guy laughed at me during my presentation, I just *felt* angry. The feelings came first; the thoughts came second."

Storytelling typically happens blindingly fast. When we believe we're at risk, we tell ourselves a story so quickly that we don't even know we're doing it. If you don't believe this is true, ask yourself whether you *always* become angry when someone

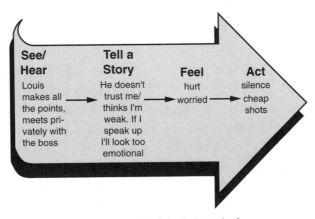

Figure 6-3.   Maria's Path to Action

laughs at you. If sometimes you do and sometimes you don't, then your response *isn't* hardwired. That means something goes on between others laughing and you feeling. In truth, you tell a story. You may not remember it, but you tell a story.

Any set of facts can be used to tell an infinite number of stories. Stories are just that, stories. These fabrications could be told in any of thousands of different ways. For instance, Maria could just as easily have decided that Louis didn't realize she cared so much about the project. She could have concluded that Louis was feeling unimportant and this was a way of showing he was valuable. Or maybe he had been burned in the past because he hadn't personally seen through every detail of a project. Any of these stories would have fit the facts and would have created very different emotions.

If we take control of our stories, they won't control us. People who excel at dialogue are able to influence their emotions during crucial conversations. They recognize that while it's true that at first we are in control of the stories we tell—after all, we do make them up of our own accord—once they're told, *the stories control us.* They control how we feel and how we act. And as a result, they control the results we get from our crucial conversations.

But it doesn't have to be this way. We can tell different stories and break the loop. In fact, *until* we tell different stories, we *cannot* break the loop.

If you want improved results from your crucial conversations, change the stories you tell yourself—even while you're in the middle of the fray.

SKILLS FOR MASTERING OUR STORIES

What's the most effective way to come up with different stories? The *best* at dialogue find a way to first slow down and then take charge of their Path to Action. Here's how.

Retrace Your Path

To slow down the lightning-quick storytelling process and the subsequent flow of adrenaline, retrace your Path to Action—one element at a time. This calls for a bit of mental gymnastics. First you have to stop what you're currently doing. Then you have to get in touch with why you're doing it. Here's how to retrace your path:

- [*Act*] Notice your behavior. Ask:

   Am I in some form of silence or violence?

- [*Feel*] Get in touch with your feelings.

   What emotions are encouraging me to act this way?

- [*Tell story*] Analyze your stories.

   What story is creating these emotions?

- [*See/hear*] Get back to the facts.

   What evidence do I have to support this story?

By retracing your path one element at a time, you put yourself in a position to think about, question, and change any one or more of the elements.

Notice Your Behavior

Why would you stop and retrace your Path to Action in the first place? Certainly if you're constantly stopping what you're doing and looking for your underlying motive and thoughts, you won't even be able to put on your shoes without thinking about it for who knows how long. You'll die of analysis paralysis.

Actually, you shouldn't constantly stop and question your actions. If you Learn to Look (as we suggested in Chapter 4) and note that you yourself are slipping into silence or violence, you have good reason to stop and take stock.

But looking isn't enough. You must take an *honest* look at what you're doing. If you tell yourself a story that your violent behavior is a "necessary tactic," you won't see the need to reconsider your actions. If you immediately jump in with "they started it," or otherwise find yourself rationalizing your behavior, you also won't feel compelled to change. Rather than stop and review what you're doing, you'll devote your time to justifying your actions to yourself and others.

When an unhelpful story is driving you to silence or violence, stop and consider how others would see your actions. For example, if the *60 Minutes* camera crew replayed this scene on national television, how would you look? What would *they* tell about your behavior?

Not only do those who are best at crucial conversations notice when they're slipping into silence or violence, but they are also able to admit it. They don't wallow in self-doubt, of course, but they do recognize the problem and begin to take corrective action. The moment they realize that they're killing dialogue, they review their own Path to Action.

Get In Touch with Your Feelings

As skilled individuals begin to retrace their own Path to Action, they immediately move from examining their own unhealthy behavior to exploring their feelings or emotions. At first glance this task sounds easy. "I'm angry!" you think to yourself. What could be easier?

Actually, identifying your emotions is more difficult than you might imagine. In fact, many people are emotionally illiterate. When asked to describe how they're feeling, they use words such as "bad" or "angry" or "frightened"—which would be okay if these were accurate descriptors, but often they're not. Individuals say they're angry when, in fact, they're feeling a mix of embarrassment and surprise. Or they suggest they're unhappy when they're feeling violated. Perhaps they suggest they're upset when they're really feeling humiliated and cheated.

Since life doesn't consist of a series of vocabulary tests, you might wonder what difference words can make. But words do matter. Knowing what you're really feeling helps you take a more accurate look at what is going on and why. For instance, you're far more likely to take an honest look at the story you're telling yourself if you admit you're feeling both embarrassed and surprised rather than simply angry.

How about you? When experiencing strong emotions, do you stop and think about your feelings? If so, do you use a rich vocabulary, or do you mostly draw from terms such as "bummed out" and "furious"? Second, do you talk openly with others about how you feel? Do you willingly talk with loved ones about what's going on inside of you? Third, in so doing, is your vocabulary robust and accurate?

It's important to get in touch with your feelings, and to do so, you may want to expand your emotional vocabulary.

Analyze Your Stories

Question your feelings and stories. Once you've identified what you're feeling, you have to stop and ask, given the circumstances, is it the *right* feeling? Meaning, of course, are you telling the right story? After all, feelings come from stories, and stories are our own invention.

The first step to regaining emotional control is to challenge the illusion that what you're feeling is the only *right* emotion under the circumstances. This may be the hardest step, but it's also the most important one. By questioning our feelings, we open ourselves up to question our stories. We challenge the comfortable conclusion that our story is right and true. We willingly question whether our emotions (very real), and the story behind them (only one of many possible explanations), are accurate.

For instance, what were the facts in Maria's story? She *saw* Louis give the whole presentation. She *heard* the boss talk about meeting with Louis to discuss the project when she wasn't present. That was the beginning of Maria's Path to Action.

Don't confuse stories with facts. Sometimes you fail to question your stories because you see them as immutable facts. When you generate stories in the blink of an eye, you can get so caught up in the moment that you begin to believe your stories are facts. They *feel* like facts. You confuse subjective conclusions with steel-hard data points. For example, in trying to ferret out facts from story, Maria might say, "He's a male chauvinist pig—that's a fact! Ask anyone who has seen how he treats me!"

"He's a male chauvinist pig" is not a fact. It's the story that Maria created to give meaning to the facts. The facts could mean just about anything. As we said earlier, others could watch Maria's interactions with Louis and walk away with different stories.

Get Back to the Facts

Separate fact from story by focusing on behavior. To separate fact from story, get back to the genuine source of your feelings. Test your ideas against a simple criterion: Can you *see* or *hear* this thing you're calling a fact? Was it an actual behavior?

For example, it is a fact that Louis "gave 95 percent of the presentation and answered all but one question." This is specific, objective, and verifiable. Any two people watching the meeting would make the same observation. However, the statement "He doesn't trust me" is a conclusion. It explains what you *think*, not what the other person *did*. Conclusions are subjective.

Spot the story by watching for "hot" words. Here's another tip. To avoid confusing story with fact, watch for "hot" terms. For example, when assessing the facts, you might say, "She scowled at me" or "He made a sarcastic comment." Words such as "scowl" and "sarcastic" are hot terms. They express judgments and attributions that, in turn, create strong emotions. They are story, not fact. Notice how much different it is when you say: "Her eyes pinched shut and her lips tightened," as opposed to "She scowled at me." In Maria's case, she suggested that Louis was controlling and didn't respect her. Had she focused on his behavior (he talked a lot and met with the boss one-on-one), this less volatile description would have allowed for any number of interpretations. For example, perhaps Louis was nervous, concerned, or unsure of himself.

Watch for Three "Clever" Stories

As we begin to piece together why people are doing what they're doing (or equally important, why we're doing what we're doing), with time and experience we become quite good at coming up with explanations that serve us well. Either our stories are completely accurate and propel us in healthy directions, or they're quite inaccurate but justify our current behavior—making us feel good about ourselves and calling for no need to change.

It's the second kind of story that routinely gets us into trouble. For example, we move to silence or violence, and then we come up with a perfectly plausible reason for why it's okay. "Of course I yelled at him. Did you see what he did? He deserved it." "Hey, don't be giving me the evil eye. I had no other choice." We call these imaginative and self-serving concoctions "clever stories." They're clever because they allow us to feel good about behaving badly. Better yet, they allow us to feel good about behaving badly even while achieving abysmal results.

Among all of the clever stories we tell, here are the three most common.

Victim Stories—"It's Not My Fault"

The first of the clever stories is a *Victim Story*. Victim Stories, as you might imagine, make us out to be innocent sufferers. The theme is always the same. The other person is bad and wrong, and we are good and right. Other people do bad things, and we suffer as a result.

In truth, there is such a thing as an innocent victim. You're stopped in the street and held up at gunpoint. When an event such as this occurs, it's a sad fact, not a story. You *are* a victim.

But all tales of victimization are not so one-sided. When you tell a Victim Story, you ignore the role you played in the problem. You tell your story in a way that judiciously avoids facts about whatever *you* have done (or neglected to do) that might have contributed to the problem.

For instance, last week your boss took you off a big project, and it hurt your feelings. You complained to everyone about how bad you felt. Of course, you failed to let your boss know that you were behind on an important project, leaving him high and dry—which is why he removed you in the first place. This part of the story you leave out because, hey, he made you feel bad.

To help support your Victim Stories you speak of nothing but your noble motives. "I took longer because I was trying to beat the standard specs." Then you tell yourself that you're being punished for your virtues, not your vices. "He just doesn't appreciate a person with my superb attention to detail." (This added twist turns you from victim into martyr. What a bonus!)

Villain Stories—"It's All Your Fault"

We create these nasty little tales by turning normal, decent human beings into villains. We impute bad motive, and then we tell everyone about the evils of the other party as if somehow we're doing the world a huge favor.

For example, we describe a boss who is zealous about quality as a control freak. When our spouse is upset that *we* didn't keep a commitment, we see him or her as inflexible and stubborn.

In Victim Stories we exaggerate our own innocence. In Villain

Stories we overemphasize the other person's guilt. We automatically assume the worst possible motives while ignoring any possible good or neutral intentions a person may have. Labeling is a common device in Villain Stories. For example, "I can't believe that *bonehead* gave me bad materials again." By employing the handy label, we are now dealing not with a complex human being, but with a bonehead.

Not only do Villain Stories help us blame others for bad results, but they also set us up to then do whatever we want to the "villains." After all, we can feel okay insulting or abusing a *bonehead*—whereas we might have to be more careful with a living, breathing person. Then when we fail to get the results we really want, we stay stuck in our ineffective behavior because, after all, look who we're dealing with!

Watch for the double standard. When you pay attention to Victim and Villain Stories and catch them for what they are—unfair characterizations—you begin to see the terrible double standard we use when our emotions are out of control. When *we* make mistakes, we tell a Victim Story by claiming our intentions were innocent and pure. "Sure I was late getting home and didn't call you, but I couldn't let the team down!" On the other hand, when *others* do things that hurt us, we tell Villain Stories in which we *invent* terrible motives for others based on how their actions affected us. "You are so thoughtless! You could have called me and told me you were going to be late."

Helpless Stories—"There's Nothing Else I Can Do"

Finally come *Helpless Stories*. In these fabrications we make ourselves out to be powerless to do anything. We convince ourselves that there are no healthy alternatives for dealing with our predicament, which justifies the action we're about to take. A Helpless Story might suggest, "If I didn't yell at my son, he wouldn't listen." Or on the flip side, "If I told my husband this, he would just be defensive." While Villian and Victim Stories look back to explain why we're in the situation we're in, Helpless Stories look forward to explain why we can't do anything to change our situation.

It's particularly easy to act helpless when we turn others' behavior into fixed and unchangeable traits. For example, when we decide our boss is a "control freak" (Villain Story), we are less inclined to give him feedback because, after all, control freaks like him don't accept feedback (Helpless Story). Nothing we can do will change that fact.

As you can see, Helpless Stories often stem from Villain Stories and typically offer us nothing more than Sucker's Choices.

Why We Tell Clever Stories

They match reality. Sometimes the stories we tell are accurate. The other person is trying to cause us harm, we are innocent victims, or maybe we really can't do much about the problem. It can happen. It's not common, but it can happen.

They get us off the hook. More often than not, our conclusions transform from reasonable explanations to clever stories when they conveniently excuse us from any responsibility—when, in reality, we have been partially responsible. The other person isn't bad and wrong, and we aren't right and good. The truth lies somewhere in the middle. However, if we can make others out as wrong and ourselves out as right, we're off the hook. Better yet, once we've demonized others, we can even insult and abuse them if we want.

Clever stories keep us from acknowledging our own sellouts. By now it should be clear that clever stories cause us problems. A reasonable question at this point is, "If they're so terribly hurtful, why do we *ever* tell clever stories?"

Our need to tell clever stories often starts with our own sellouts. Like it or not, we usually don't begin telling stories that justify our actions until we have done something that we feel a need to justify.[1]

We sell out when we consciously act against our own sense of what's right. And after we've sold out, we have only two choices: own up to our sellout, or try to justify it. And if we don't admit to our errors, we inevitably look for ways to justify them. That's when we begin to tell clever stories.

Let's look at an example of a sellout: You're driving in heavy traffic. You begin to pass cars that are attempting to merge into your lane. A car very near you has accelerated and is entering your lane. A thought strikes you that you *should* let him in. It's the nice thing to do, and you'd want someone to let you in. But you don't. You accelerate forward and close the gap. What happens next? You begin to have thoughts like these: "He can't just crowd in on me. What a jerk! I've been fighting this traffic a long time. Besides, I've got an important appointment to get to." And so on.

This story makes you the innocent victim and the other person the nasty villain. Under the influence of this story you now feel justified in not doing what you originally thought you should have done. You also ignore what you would think of others who did the same thing—"That jerk didn't let me in!"

Consider an example more related to crucial conversations. Your spouse has an annoying habit. It's not a big deal, but you feel you should mention it. But you don't. Instead, you just huff or roll your eyes, hoping that will send the message. Unfortunately, your spouse doesn't pick up the hint and continues the habit. Your annoyance turns to resentment. You feel disgusted that your spouse is so thick that he or she can't pick up an obvious hint. And besides, you shouldn't have to mention this anyway—any reasonable person should notice this on his or her own! Do you have to point out *everything*? From this point forward you begin to make insulting wisecracks about the issue until it escalates into an ugly confrontation.

Notice the order of the events in both of these examples. What came first, the story or the sellout? Did you convince yourself of the other driver's selfishness and *then* not let him in? Of course not. You had no reason to think he was selfish until you needed an excuse for your own selfish behavior. You didn't start telling clever stories until *after* you failed to do something you knew you should have done. Your spouse's annoying habit didn't become a source of resentment until you became part of the problem. You got upset because you sold out. And the clever story helped you feel good about being rude.

Sellouts are often not big events. In fact, they can be so small that they're easy for us to overlook when we're crafting our clever stories. Here are some common ones:

- You believe you should help someone, but don't.

- You believe you should apologize, but don't.

- You believe you should stay late to finish up on a commitment, but go home instead.

- You say yes when you know you should say no, then hope no one follows up to see if you keep your commitment.

- You believe you should talk to someone about concerns you have with him or her, but don't.

- You do less than your share and think you should acknowledge it, but say nothing knowing no one else will bring it up either.

- You believe you should listen respectfully to feedback, but become defensive instead.

- You see problems with a plan someone presents and think you should speak up, but don't.

- You fail to complete an assignment on time and believe you should let others know, but don't.

- You know you have information a coworker could use, but keep it to yourself.

Even small sellouts like these get us started telling clever stories. When we don't admit to our own mistakes, we obsess about others' faults, our innocence, and our powerlessness to do anything other than what we're already doing. We tell a clever story when we want self-justification more than results. Of course, self-justification is not what we *really* want, but we certainly act as if it is.

With that sad fact in mind, let's focus on what we really want. Let's look at the final Master My Stories skill.

Tell the Rest of the Story

Once we've learned to recognize the clever stories we tell ourselves, we can move to the final Master My Stories skill. The dialogue-smart recognize that they're telling clever stories, stop, and then do what it takes to tell a *useful* story. A useful story, by definition, creates emotions that lead to healthy action—such as dialogue.

And what transforms a clever story into a useful one? The rest of the story. That's because clever stories have one characteristic in common: They're incomplete. Clever stories omit crucial information about us, about others, and about our options. Only by including all of these essential details can clever stories be transformed into useful ones.

What's the best way to fill in the missing details? Quite simply, it's done by turning victims into actors, villains into humans, and the helpless into the able. Here's how.

Turn victims into actors. If you notice that you're talking about yourself as an innocent victim (and you weren't held up at gunpoint), ask:

- Am I pretending not to notice my role in the problem?

This question jars you into facing up to the fact that maybe, just maybe, you did something to help cause the problem. Instead of being a victim, you were an actor. This doesn't necessarily mean you had malicious motives. Perhaps your contribution was merely a thoughtless omission. Nonetheless, you contributed.

For example, a coworker constantly leaves the harder or noxious tasks for you to complete. You've frequently complained to friends and loved ones about being exploited. The parts you leave out of the story are that you smile broadly when your boss compliments you for your willingness to take on challenging jobs, and you've never said anything to your coworker. You've hinted, but that's about it.

The first step in telling the rest of this story would be to add these important facts to your account. By asking what role you've played, you begin to realize how selective your perception has been. You become aware of how you've minimized your own mistakes while you've exaggerated the role of others.

Turn villains into humans. When you find yourself labeling or otherwise vilifying others, stop and ask:

- Why would a reasonable, rational, and decent person do what this person is doing?

This particular question humanizes others. As we search for plausible answers to it, our emotions soften. Empathy often replaces judgment, and depending upon how *we've* treated *others*, personal accountability replaces self-justification.

For instance, that coworker who seems to conveniently miss out on the tough jobs told you recently that she could see you were struggling with an important assignment, and yesterday (while you were tied up on a pressing task) she pitched in and completed the job for you. You were instantly suspicious. She was trying to make you look bad by completing a high-profile job. How dare she pretend to be helpful when her real goal was to discredit you while tooting her own horn! Well, that's the story you've told yourself.

But what if she really were a reasonable, rational, and decent person? What if she had no motive other than to give you a hand? Isn't it a bit early to be vilifying her? And if you do, don't you run the risk of ruining a relationship? Might you go off half-cocked, accuse her, and then learn you were wrong?

Our purpose for asking why a reasonable, rational, and decent person might be acting a certain way is *not* to excuse others for any bad things they may be doing. If they are, indeed, guilty, we'll have time to deal with that later. The purpose of the humanizing question is to deal with our own stories and emotions. It provides us with still another tool for working on ourselves first by providing a variety of possible reasons for the other person's behavior.

In fact, with experience and maturity we learn to worry less about others' intent and more about the *effect* others' actions are having on us. No longer are we in the game of rooting out unhealthy motives. And here's the good news. When we reflect on alternative motives, not only do we soften our emotions, but equally important, we relax our absolute certainty long enough to allow for dialogue—the only reliable way of discovering others' genuine motives.

Turn the helpless into the able. Finally, when you catch yourself bemoaning your own helplessness, you can tell the complete story by returning to your original motive. To do so, stop and ask:

- What do I really want? For me? For others? For the relationship?

Then, kill the Sucker's Choice that's made you feel helpless to choose anything other than silence or violence. Do this by asking:

- What would I do right now if I really wanted these results?

For example, you now find yourself insulting your coworker for not pitching in with a tough job. Your coworker seems surprised at your strong and "out of the blue" reaction. In fact, she's staring at you as if you've slipped a cog. You, of course, have told yourself that she is purposefully avoiding noxious tasks, and that despite your helpful hints, she has made no changes.

"I have to get brutal," you tell yourself. "I don't like it, but if I don't offend her, I'll be stuck doing the grunt work forever."

You've strayed from what you really want—to share work equally *and* to have a good relationship. You've given up on half of your goals by making a Sucker's Choice. "Oh well, better to offend her than to be made a fool."

What should you be doing instead? Openly, honestly, and effectively discussing the problem—not taking potshots and then justifying yourself. When you refuse to make yourself helpless, you're forced to hold yourself accountable for using your dialogue skills rather than bemoaning your weakness.

MARIA'S NEW STORY

To see how this all fits together, let's circle back to Maria. Let's assume she's retraced her Path to Action and separated the facts from the stories. Doing this has helped her realize that the story she told was incomplete, defensive, and hurtful. When she watched for the Three Clever Stories, she saw them with painful clarity. Now she's ready to tell the rest of the story. So she asks herself:

- Am I pretending not to notice my role in the problem?

  "When I found out that Louis was holding project meetings without me, I felt like I should ask him about why I wasn't included. I believed that if I did, I could open a dialogue that would help us work better together. But then I didn't, and as

my resentment grew, I was even less interested in broaching the subject."

- Why would a reasonable, rational, and decent person do what Louis is doing?

"He really cares about producing good-quality work. Maybe he doesn't realize that I'm as committed to the success of the project as he is."

- What do I really want?

"I want a respectful relationship with Louis. And I want recognition for the work I do."

- What would I do right now if I really wanted these results?

"I'd make an appointment to sit down with Louis and talk about how we work together."

As we tell the rest of the story, we free ourselves from the poisoning effects of unhealthy emotions. Best of all, as we regain control and move back to dialogue, we become masters of our own emotions rather than hostages.

And what about Maria? What did she actually do? She scheduled a meeting with Louis. As she prepared for the meeting, she refused to feed her ugly and incomplete stories, admitted her own role in the problem, and entered the conversation with an open mind. Perhaps Louis wasn't trying to make her appear bad or fill in for her incompetence.

As Maria sat down with Louis, she found a way to tentatively share what she had observed. (We'll look at exactly how to do this in the next chapter.) Fortunately, not only did Maria master her story, but she knew how to talk about it as well. While engaging in healthy dialogue, Louis apologized for not including her in meetings with the boss. He explained that he was trying to give the boss a heads-up on some controversial parts of the presentation—and realized in retrospect that he shouldn't have done this without her. He also apologized for dominating during the presentation. Maria learned from the conversation that Louis tends to talk more when he gets nervous. He suggested that they each be responsible for either the first or second half of the presentation and stick to their assignments so he would be less likely to crowd her out. The discussion ended with both of them understanding the other's perspective and Louis promising to be more sensitive in the future.

SUMMARY—MASTER MY STORIES

If strong emotions are keeping you stuck in silence or violence, try this.

Retrace Your Path

Notice your behavior. If you find yourself moving away from dialogue, ask yourself what you're really doing.

- Am I in some form of silence or violence?

Get in touch with your feelings. Learn to accurately identify the emotions behind your story.

- What emotions are encouraging me to act this way?

Analyze your stories. Question your conclusions and look for other possible explanations behind your story.

- What story is creating these emotions?

Get back to the facts. Abandon your absolute certainty by distinguishing between hard facts and your invented story.

- What evidence do I have to support this story?

Watch for clever stories. Victim, Villain, and Helpless Stories sit at the top of the list.

Tell the Rest of the Story

Ask:

- Am I pretending not to notice my role in the problem?
- Why would a reasonable, rational, and decent person do this?
- What do I really want?
- What would I do right now if I really wanted these results?

7

Outspoken by whom?

—DOROTHY PARKER
WHEN TOLD THAT SHE WAS VERY OUTSPOKEN

STATE My Path

How to Speak Persuasively, Not Abrasively

So far we've gone to great pains to prepare ourselves for crucial conversations. Here's what we've learned. Our hearts need to be in the right place. We need to pay close attention to crucial conversations—particularly when people start feeling unsafe. And heaven forbid that we should tell ourselves clever and unhelpful stories.

So let's say that we are well prepared. We're ready to open our mouths and start sharing our pool of meaning. That's right, we're actually going to talk. Now what?

Most of the time we walk into a discussion and slide into autopilot. "Hi, how are the kids? What's going on at work?" What could be easier than talking? We know thousands of words and generally weave them into conversations that suit our needs. Most of the time.

However, when stakes rise and our emotions kick in, well, that's when we open our mouths and don't do so well. In fact, as we suggested earlier, the more important the discussion, the less likely we are to be on our best behavior. More specifically, we advocate or express our views quite poorly.

To help us improve our advocacy skills, we'll examine two challenging situations. First, we'll look at five skills for talking when what we have to say could easily make others defensive. Second, we'll explore how these same skills help us state our opinions when we believe so strongly in something that we risk shutting others down rather than opening them up to our ideas.

SHARING RISKY MEANING

Adding information to the pool of meaning can be quite difficult when the ideas we're about to dump into the collective consciousness contain delicate, unattractive, or controversial opinions.

> "I'm sorry, Marta, but people simply don't like working with you. You've been asked to leave the special-projects team."

It's one thing to argue that your company needs to shift from green to red packaging; it's quite another to tell a person that he or she is offensive or unlikable or has a controlling leadership style. When the topic turns from things to people, it's always more difficult, and to nobody's surprise, some people are better at it than others.

When it comes to sharing touchy information, the *worst* alternate between bluntly dumping their ideas into the pool and saying nothing at all. Either they start with: "You're not going to like this, but, hey, somebody has to be honest . . ." (a classic Sucker's Choice), or they simply stay mum.

Fearful they could easily destroy a healthy relationship, those who are *good* at dialogue say some of what's on their minds but understate their views out of fear of hurting others. They talk, but they sugarcoat their message.

The *best* at dialogue speak their minds completely and do it in a way that makes it safe for others to hear what they have to say and respond to it as well. They are both totally frank and completely respectful.

MAINTAIN SAFETY

In order to speak honestly when honesty could easily offend others, we have to find a way to maintain safety. That's a bit like telling someone to smash another person in the nose, but, you know, don't hurt him. How can we speak the unspeakable and still maintain respect? Actually, it can be done if you know how to carefully blend three ingredients—confidence, humility, and skill.

Confidence. Most people simply won't hold delicate conversations—well, at least not with the right person. For instance, your colleague Brian goes home at night and tells his wife that his boss, Fernando, is micromanaging him to within an inch of his life. He says the same thing over lunch when talking with his pals. Everyone knows what Brian thinks about Fernando—except, of course, Fernando.

People who are skilled at dialogue have the confidence to say what needs to be said to the person who needs to hear it. They are confident that their opinions deserve to be placed in the pool of meaning. They are also confident that they can speak openly without brutalizing others or causing undue offense.

Humility. Confidence does not equate to arrogance or pigheadedness. Skilled people are confident that they have something to say, but also realize that others have valuable input. They are humble enough to realize that they don't have a monopoly on the truth. Their opinions provide a starting point but not the final word. They may currently believe something but realize that with new information they may change their minds. This means they're willing to both express their opinions and encourage others to do the same

Skill. Finally, people who willingly share delicate information are good at doing it. That's why they're confident in the first place. They don't make a Sucker's Choice because they've found a path that allows for both candor and safety. They speak the unspeakable, and people are grateful for their honesty.

Good Night and Good-Bye!

To see how to discuss sensitive issues, let's look at an enormously difficult problem. Bob has just walked in the door, and his wife, Carole, looks upset. He can tell from her swollen eyes that she's been crying. Only when he walks in the door, Carole doesn't turn to him for comfort. Instead, she looks at him with an expression that says "How could you?" Bob doesn't know it yet, but Carole thinks he's having an affair. He's not.

How did Carole come to this dangerous and wrong conclusion? Earlier that day she had been going over the credit card statement when she noticed a charge from the Good Night Motel—a cheap place located not more than a mile from their home. "Why would he stay in a motel so close to home?" she wonders. "And why didn't I know about it?" Then it hits her— "That unfaithful jerk!"

Now what's the worst way Carole might handle this (one that doesn't involve packing up and moving back to Wisconsin)? What's the worst way of *talking* about the problem? Most people agree that jumping in with an ugly accusation followed by a threat is a good candidate for that distinction. It's also what most people do, and Carole is no exception.

"I can't believe you're doing this to me," she says in a painful tone.

"Doing what?" Bob asks—not knowing what she's talking about but figuring that whatever it is, it can't be good.

"You know what I'm talking about," she says, continuing to keep Bob on edge.

"Do I need to apologize for missing her birthday?" Bob wonders to himself. "No, it's not even summer and her birthday is on . . . well, it's sweltering on her birthday."

"I'm sorry, I don't know what you're talking about," he responds, taken aback.

"You're having an affair, and I have proof right here!" Carole explains holding up a piece of crumpled paper.

"What's on that paper that says I'm having an affair?" he asks, completely befuddled because (1) he's not having an affair and (2) the paper contains not a single compromising photo.

"It's a motel bill, you jerk. You take some woman to a motel, and you put it on the credit card?! I can't believe you're doing this to me!"

Now if Carole were certain that Bob was having an affair, perhaps this kind of talk would be warranted. It may not be the best way to work through the issue, but Bob would at least understand why Carole made the accusations and hurled threats.

But, in truth, she only has a piece of paper with some numbers on it. This tangible piece of evidence has made her suspicious. How should she talk about this nasty hunch in a way that leads to dialogue?

STATE MY PATH

If Carole's goal is to have a healthy conversation about a tough topic (e.g., I think you're having an affair), her only hope is to stay in dialogue. That holds true for anybody with any crucial conversation (i.e., It feels like you micromanage me; I fear you're using drugs). That means that despite your worst suspicions, you shouldn't violate respect. In a similar vein, you shouldn't kill safety with threats and accusations.

So what should you do? Start with Heart. Think about what you *really* want and how dialogue can help you get it. And master your story—realize that you may be jumping to a hasty Victim, Villain, or Helpless Story. The best way to find out the true story is not to *act out* the worst story you can generate. That will lead to self-destructive silence and violence games. Think about other possible explanations long enough to temper your emotions so you can get to dialogue. Besides, if it turns out you're right about your initial impression, there will be plenty of time for confrontations later on.

Once you've worked on yourself to create the right conditions for dialogue, you can then draw upon five distinct skills that can help you talk about even the most sensitive topics. These five tools can be easily remembered with the acronym STATE. It stands for:

- Share your facts
- Tell your story
- Ask for others' paths
- Talk tentatively
- Encourage testing

The first three skills describe *what* to do. The last two tell *how* to do it.

The "What" Skills

Share Your Facts

In the last chapter we suggested that if you retrace your Path to Action to the source, you eventually arrive at the facts. For example, Carole found the credit card invoice. That's a fact. She then told a story—Bob's having an affair. Next, she felt betrayed and horrified. Finally, she attacked Bob—"I should never have married you!" The whole interaction was fast, predictable, and very ugly.

What if Carole took a different route—one that started with facts? What if she were able to suspend the ugly story she told herself (perhaps think of an alternative story) and then start her conversation with the facts? Wouldn't that be a safer way to go? "Maybe," she muses, "there is a good reason behind all of this. Why don't I start with the suspicious bill and then go from there?"

If she started there, she'd be right. The best way to share your view is to follow your Path to Action from beginning to end— the same way you traveled it (Figure 7-1). Unfortunately, when we're drunk on adrenaline, our tendency is to do precisely the opposite. Since we're obsessing on our emotions and stories, that's what we start with. Of course, this is the most controversial, least influential, and most insulting way we could begin.

To make matters worse, this strategy creates still another self-fulfilling prophecy. We're so anxious to blurt out our ugly stories

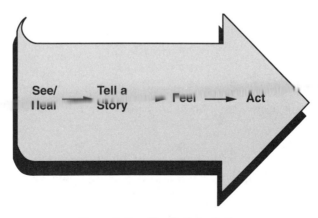

Figure 7-1.   The Path to Action

that we say things in extremely ineffective ways. Then, when we get bad results (and we *are* going to get bad results), we tell ourselves that we just can't share risky views without creating problems. So the next time we've got something sticky to say, we're even more reluctant to say it. We hold it inside where the story builds up steam, and when we do eventually share our horrific story, we do so with a vengeance. The cycle starts all over again.

Facts are the least controversial. Facts provide a safe beginning. By their very nature, facts aren't controversial. That's why we call them facts. For example, consider the statement: "Yesterday you arrived at work twenty minutes late." No dispute there. Conclusions, on the other hand, are highly controversial. For example: "You can't be trusted." That's hardly a fact. Actually, it's more like an insult, and it can certainly be disputed. Eventually we may want to share our conclusions, but we certainly don't want to open up with a controversy.

Facts are the most persuasive. In addition to being less controversial, facts are also more persuasive than subjective conclusions. Facts form the foundation of belief. So if you want to persuade others, don't start with your stories. Start with your observations. For example, which of the following do you find more persuasive?

"I want you to stop sexually harassing me!"

or

"When you talk to me, your eyes move up and down rather than look at my face. And sometimes you put your hand on my shoulder."

While we're speaking here about being persuasive, let's add that our goal is not to persuade others that we are *right*. We aren't trying to "win" the dialogue. We just want our meaning to get a fair hearing. We're trying to help others see how a reasonable, rational, and decent person could end up with the story we're carrying. That's all.

When we start with shocking or offensive conclusions ("Quit groping me with your eyes!" or "I think we should declare bankruptcy"), we actually encourage others to tell Villain Stories about us. Since we've given them no facts to support our conclusion, they make up reasons we're saying these things. They're likely to believe we're either stupid or evil.

So if your goal is to help others see how a reasonable, rational, and decent person could think what you're thinking, start with your facts.

And if you aren't sure what your facts are (your story is absolutely filling your brain), take the time to think them through *before* you enter the crucial conversation. Take the time to sort out facts from conclusions. Gathering the facts is the homework required for crucial conversations.

Facts are the least insulting. If you do want to share your story, don't start with it. Your story (particularly if it has led to a rather ugly conclusion) could easily surprise and insult others. It could kill safety in one rash, ill-conceived sentence.

BRIAN: I'd like to talk to you about your leadership style.
You micromanage me, and it's starting to drive me nuts.

FERNANDO: What? I ask you if you're going to be done on time and you lay into me with . . .

If you start with your story (and in so doing, kill safety), you may never actually get to the facts.

Begin your path with facts. In order to talk about your stories, you need to lead the others involved down your Path to Action. Let them experience your path from the beginning to the end, and not from the end to—well, to wherever it takes you. Let others see your experience from your point of view—starting with your facts. This way, when you do talk about what you're starting to conclude, they'll understand why. First the facts, then the story—and then make sure that as you explain your story, you tell it as a possible story, not as concrete fact.

> BRIAN: Since I started work here, you've asked to meet with me twice a day. That's more than with anyone else. You have also asked me to pass all of my ideas by you before I include them in a project. [*The facts*]

> FERNANDO: What's your point?

> BRIAN: I'm not sure that you're intending to send this message, but I'm beginning to wonder if you don't trust me. Maybe you think I'm not up to the job or that I'll get you into trouble. Is that what's going on? [*The* possible *story*]

> FERNANDO: Really, I was merely trying to give you a chance to get my input before you got too far down the path on a project. The last guy I worked with was constantly taking his project to near completion only to learn that he'd left out a key element. I'm trying to avoid surprises.

Earn the right to share your story by starting with your facts. Facts lay the groundwork for all delicate conversations.

Tell Your Story

Sharing your story can be tricky. Even if you've started with your facts, the other person can still become defensive when you move from facts to stories. After all, you're sharing potentially unflattering conclusions and judgments.

Why share your story in the first place? Because the facts alone are rarely worth mentioning. It's the facts plus the conclusion that call for a face-to-face discussion. In addition, if you simply mention the facts, the other person may not understand the severity of the implications. For example:

"I noticed that you had company software in your brief-case."
"Yep, that's the beauty of software. It's portable."
"That particular software is proprietary."
"It ought to be! Our future depends on it."
"My understanding is that it's not supposed to go home."
"Of course not. That's how people steal it."

(*Sounds like it's time for a conclusion.*) "I was wondering what the software is doing in your briefcase. It looks like you're taking it home. Is that what's going on here?"

It takes confidence. To be honest, it can be difficult to share negative conclusions and unattractive judgments (e.g., "I'm wondering if you're a thief"). It takes confidence to share such a potentially inflammatory story. However, if you've done your homework by thinking through the facts behind your story you'll realize that you *are* drawing a reasonable, rational, and decent conclusion. One that deserves hearing. And by starting with the facts, you've laid the groundwork. By thinking through the facts and then leading with them, you're much more likely to have the confidence you need to add controversial and vitally important meaning to the shared pool.

Don't pile it on. Sometimes we lack the confidence to speak up, so we let problems simmer for a long time. Given the chance, we generate a whole arsenal of unflattering conclusions. For example, you're about to hold a crucial conversation with your child's second-grade teacher. The teacher wants to hold your daughter back a year. You want your daughter to advance right along with her age group. This is what's going on in your head:

"I can't believe this! This teacher is straight out of college, and she wants to hold Debbie back. To be perfectly frank, I don't think she gives much weight to the stigma of being held back. Worse still, she's quoting the recommendation of the school psychologist. The guy's a real idiot. I've met him, and I wouldn't trust him with a common cold. I'm not going to let these two morons push me around."

Which of these insulting conclusions or judgments should you share? Certainly not the entire menagerie of unflattering tales. In fact, you're going to need to work on this Villain Story before you have any hope of healthy dialogue. As you do, your story begins to sound more like this (note the careful choice of terms—after all, it is your story, not the facts):

"When I first heard your recommendation, my initial reaction was to oppose your decision. But after thinking about it, I've realized I could be wrong. I realized I don't really have any experience about what's best for Debbie in this situation—only fears about the stigma of being held back. I know it's a complex issue. I'd like to talk about how both of us can more objectively weigh this decision."

Look for safety problems. As you share your story, watch for signs that safety is deteriorating. If people start becoming defensive or appear to be insulted, step out of the conversation and rebuild safety by Contrasting.

Use Contrasting. Here's how it works:

"I know you care a great deal about my daughter, and I'm confident you're well-trained. That's not my concern at all. I know you want to do what's best for Debbie, and I do too. My only issue is that this is an ambiguous decision with huge implications for the rest of her life."

Be careful not to apologize for your views. Remember, the goal of Contrasting is not to water down your message, but to be sure that people don't hear more than you intend. Be confident enough to share what you really want to express.

Ask for Others' Paths

We mentioned that the key to sharing sensitive ideas is a blend of confidence and humility. We express our confidence by sharing our facts and stories clearly. We demonstrate our humility by then asking others to share their views.

So once you've shared your point of view—facts and stories alike—invite others to do the same. If your goal is to learn rather than to be right, to make the best decision rather than to get your way, then you'll be willing to hear other views. By being open to learning we are demonstrating humility at its best.

For example, ask yourself: "What does the schoolteacher think?" "Is your boss really intending to micromanage you?" "Is your spouse really having an affair?"

To find out others' views on the matter, encourage them to express their facts, stories, and feelings. Then carefully listen to what they have to say. Equally important, be willing to abandon or reshape your story as more information pours into the Pool of Shared Meaning.

The "How" Skills

Talk Tentatively

If you look back at the vignettes we've shared so far, you'll note that we were careful to describe both facts and stories in a tentative way. For example, "I was wondering why . . ."

Talking tentatively simply means that we tell our story as a story rather than disguising it as a fact. "Perhaps you were unaware . . ." suggests that you're not absolutely certain. "In my opinion . . ." says you're sharing an opinion and no more.

When sharing a story, strike a blend between confidence and humility. Share in a way that expresses appropriate confidence in your conclusions while demonstrating that, if appropriate, you want your conclusions challenged. To do so, change "The fact is" to "In my opinion." Swap "Everyone knows that" for "I've talked to three of our suppliers who think that." Soften "It's clear to me" to "I'm beginning to wonder if."

Why soften the message? Because we're trying to add meaning to the pool, not force it down other people's throats. If we're too forceful, the information won't make it into the pool. Besides, with both facts and stories, we're *not* absolutely certain they're true. Our observations could be faulty. Our stories— well, they're only educated guesses.

In addition, when we use tentative language, not only does it accurately portray our uncertain view, but it also helps reduce defensiveness and makes it safe for others to offer differing opinions. One of the ironies of dialogue is that when we're sharing controversial ideas with potentially resistant people, the more forceful we are, the less persuasive we are. In short, talking tentatively can actually increase our influence.

Tentative, not wimpy. Some people are so worried about being too forceful or pushy that they err in the other direction. They wimp out by making still another Sucker's Choice. They figure that the only safe way to share touchy data is to act as if it's not important.

"I know this is probably not true . . ." or "Call me crazy but . . ."

When you begin with a complete disclaimer and do it in a tone that suggests you're consumed with doubt, you do the message a disservice. It's one thing to be humble and open. It's quite another to be clinically uncertain. Use language that says you're sharing an opinion, not language that says you're a nervous wreck.

A "Good" Story—The Goldilocks Test

To get a feel for how to best share your story, making sure that you're neither too hard nor too soft, consider the following examples:

Too soft: "This is probably stupid, but . . ."

Too hard: "How come you ripped us off?"

Just right: "It's starting to look like you're taking this home for your own use. Is that right?"

Too soft: "I'm ashamed to even mention this, but . . ."

Too hard: "Just when did you start using hard drugs?"

Just right: "It's leading me to conclude that you're starting to use drugs. Do you have another explanation that I'm missing here?"

Too soft: "It's probably my fault, but . . ."

Too hard: "You wouldn't trust your own mother to make a one-minute egg!"

Just right: "I'm starting to feel like you don't trust me. Is that what's going on here? If so, I'd like to know what I did to lose your trust."

Too soft: "Maybe I'm just oversexed or something, but . . ."

Too hard: "If you don't find a way to pick up the frequency, I'm walking."

Just right: "I don't think you're intending this, but I'm beginning to feel rejected."

Encourage Testing

When you ask others to share their paths, how you phrase your invitation makes a big difference. Not only should you invite others to talk, but you have to do so in a way that makes it clear that no matter how controversial their ideas are, you want to hear them. Others need to feel safe sharing their observations and stories—even if they differ. Otherwise, they don't speak up and you can't test the accuracy and relevance of your views.

This becomes particularly important when you're having a crucial conversation with people who might move to silence. Some people make Sucker's Choices in these circumstances. They worry that if they share their true opinions, others will clam up. So they choose between speaking their minds and hearing others out. But the *best* at dialogue don't choose. They do both. They understand that the only limit to how strongly you can express your opinion is your willingness to be equally vigorous in encouraging others to challenge it.

Invite opposing views. So if you think others may be hesitant, make it clear that you want to hear their views—no matter their opinion. If they disagree, so much the better. If what they have to say is controversial or even touchy, respect them for finding the courage to express what they're thinking. If they have different facts or stories, you need to hear them to help complete the picture. Make sure they have the opportunity to share by actively inviting them to do so: "Does anyone see it differently?" "What am I missing here?" "I'd really like to hear the other side of this story."

Mean it. Sometimes people offer an invitation that sounds more like a threat than a legitimate call for opinions. "Well, that's how I see it. Nobody disagrees, do they?" Invite people with both words and tone that say "I really want to hear from you." For instance: "I know people have been reluctant to speak up about this, but I would really love to hear from everyone."

Or: "I know there are at least two sides to this story. Could we hear differing views now? What problems could this decision cause us?"

Play devil's advocate. Occasionally you can tell that others are not buying into your facts or story, but they're not speaking up either. You've sincerely invited them, even encouraged differing views, but nobody says anything. To help grease the skids, play devil's advocate. Model disagreeing by disagreeing with your own view. "Maybe I'm wrong here. What if the opposite is true? What if the reason sales have dropped is because . . ."

BACK TO THE MOTEL

To see how all of the STATE skills fit together in a touchy conversation, let's return to the motel bill. Only this time, Carole does a far better job of bringing up a delicate issue.

BOB: Hi honey, how was your day?

CAROLE: Not so good.

BOB: Why's that?

CAROLE: I was checking our credit card bill, and I noticed a charge of forty-eight dollars for the Good Night Motel down the street. [*Shares facts*]

BOB: Boy, that sounds wrong.

CAROLE: It sure does.

BOB: Well, don't worry. I'll check into it one day when I'm going by.

CAROLE: I'd feel better if we checked right now.

BOB: Really? It's less than fifty bucks. It can wait.

CAROLE: It's not the money that has me worried.

BOB: You're worried?

CAROLE: It's a motel down the street. You know that's how my sister found out that Phil was having an affair. She found a suspicious hotel bill. [*Shares story—tentatively*] I don't have anything to worry about do I? What do you think is going on with this bill? [*Asks for other's path*]

BOB: I don't know, but you certainly don't have to worry about me.

CAROLE: I know that you've given me no reason to question your fidelity. I don't really believe that you're having an affair. [*Contrasting*] It's just that it might help put my mind to rest if we were to check on this right now. Would that bother you? [*Encourages testing*]

BOB: Not at all. Let's give them a call and find out what's going on.

When this conversation actually did take place, it sounded exactly like the one portrayed above. The suspicious spouse avoided nasty accusations and ugly stories, shared facts, and then tentatively shared a possible conclusion. As it turns out, the couple had gone out to a Chinese restaurant earlier that month. The owner of the restaurant also owned the motel and used the same credit card imprinting machine at both establishments. Oops.

By tentatively sharing a story rather than attacking, name-calling, and threatening, the worried spouse averted a huge battle, and the couple's relationship was strengthened at a time when it could easily have been damaged.

STRONG BELIEF

Now let's turn our attention to another communication challenge. This time you're not offering delicate feedback or iffy stories; you're merely going to step into an argument and advocate your point of view. It's the kind of thing you do all the time. You do it at home, you do it at work, and yes, you've even been known to fire off an opinion or two while standing in line at the DMV.

Unfortunately, as stakes rise and others argue differing views—*and you just know in your heart of hearts that you're right and they're wrong*—you start pushing too hard. You simply have to win. There's too much at risk and only you have the right ideas. Left to their own devices, others will mess things up. So when you care a great deal and are sure of your views, you don't merely speak—you try to force your opinions on others. Quite naturally, others resist. You in turn push even harder.

As consultants, we (the authors) watch this kind of thing happen all the time. For instance, seated around the table is a group of leaders who are starting to debate an important topic. First, someone hints that she's the only one with any real insight. Then someone else starts tossing out facts like so many poisonous darts. Another—it just so happens someone with critical information—retreats into silence. As emotions rise, words that were once carefully chosen and tentatively delivered are now spouted with an absolute certainty that is typically reserved for claims that are nailed to church doors or carved on stone tablets.

In the end, nobody is listening, everyone is committed to silence or violence, and the Pool of Shared Meaning is dry. Nobody wins.

How Did We Get Like This?

It starts with a story. When we feel the need to push our ideas on others, it's generally because we believe we're right and everyone else is wrong. There's no need to expand the pool of meaning, because we *own* the pool. We also firmly believe it's our duty to fight for the truth that we're holding. It's the honorable thing to do. It's what people of character do.

Of course, others aren't exactly villains in this story. They simply don't know any better. We, on the other hand, are modern-day heroes crusading against naiveté and tunnel vision.

We feel justified in using dirty tricks. Once we're convinced that it's our duty to fight for the truth, we start pulling out the big guns. We use debating tricks that we've picked up throughout the years. Chief among them is the ability to "stack the deck." We cite information that supports our ideas while hiding or discrediting anything that doesn't. Then we spice things up with exaggeration: "Everyone knows that this is the only way to go." When this doesn't work, we lace our language with inflammatory terms: "All right-thinking people would agree with me."

From there we employ any number of dirty tricks. We appeal to authority: "Well, that's what the boss thinks." We attack the person: "You're not so naive as to actually believe that?" We draw hasty generalizations: "If it happened in our overseas operation, it'll happen here for sure."

And again, the harder we try and the more forceful our tactics, the greater the resistance we create, the worse the results, and the more battered our relationships.

How Do We Change?

The solution to excessive advocacy is actually rather simple—if you can just bring yourself to do it. When you find yourself just dying to convince others that your way is best, back off your current attack and think about what you really want for yourself, others, and the relationship. Then ask yourself, "How would I behave if these were the results I really wanted?" When your adrenaline level gets below the 0.05 legal limit, you'll be able to use your STATE skills.

First, watch for the moment when people start to resist you. Turn your attention from the topic (no matter how important) to yourself. Are you leaning forward? Are you speaking more loudly? Are you starting to try to win? Are you speaking in lengthy monologues and using dirty tricks? Remember: *The more you care about an issue, the less likely you are to be on your best behavior.*

Second, tone down your approach. Open yourself up to the belief that others might have something to say, and better still, they might even hold a piece of the puzzle—and then ask them for their views.

Of course, this isn't easy. Backing off when we care the most is so counterintuitive that most of us have trouble pulling it off. It's not easy to soften your language when you're positive about something. And who wants to ask for other views when you know they're wrong? That's positively nuts.

In fact, it can feel disingenuous to be tentative when your own strong belief is being brought into question. Of course, when you watch *others* shift from healthy dialogue to forcing their way on others, it's obvious that if they don't back off, nobody will buy in. That's when you're watching *others*. On the other hand, when we ourselves are pushing hard, it's the correct thing to do. Right?

Let's face it. When it comes to our strongest views, passion can be our enemy. Of course, feeling strongly about something isn't bad in and of itself. It's okay to have strong opinions. The problem comes when we try to express them.

For instance, when we believe strongly in a concept or a cause, our emotions kick in and we start trying to force our way onto others. As our emotions kick in, our ideas no longer flow into the pool. Instead, our thoughts shoot out of our mouths like water out of a raging fire hydrant. And guess what—others become defensive. When this happens, when our emotions turn our ideas into a harsh and painful stream of thoughts, our honest passion kills the argument rather than supports it.

Catch yourself. So what's a person to do? Catch yourself before you launch into a monologue. Realize that if you're starting to feel indignant or if you can't figure out why others don't buy in—after all, it's so obvious to you—recognize that you're starting to enter dangerous territory.

Back off your harsh and conclusive language, not your belief. Hold to your belief; merely soften your approach.

SUMMARY—STATE MY PATH

When you have a tough message to share, or when you are so convinced of your own rightness that you may push too hard, remember to STATE your path:

- *Share your facts.* Start with the least controversial, most persuasive elements from your Path to Action.

- *Tell your story.* Explain what you're beginning to conclude.

- *Ask for others' paths.* Encourage others to share both their facts and their stories.

- *Talk tentatively.* State your story as a story—don't disguise it as a fact.

- *Encourage testing.* Make it safe for others to express differing or even opposing views.

8

Explore Others' Paths

How to Listen When Others Blow Up or Clam Up

Over the past few months your daughter Wendy has started to date a guy who looks like he's about ten minutes away from a felony arrest. After only a few weeks of dating this fellow, Wendy's clothing preference is now far too suggestive for your taste, and she routinely punctuates her language with expletives. When you carefully try to talk to her about these recent changes, she shouts accusations and insults and then withdraws to her room where she sulks for hours on end.

Now what? Should you do something given that you're not the one going to silence or violence? When others clam up (refusing to speak their minds) or blow up (communicating in a way that is abusive and insulting), is there something you can do to get them to dialogue?

The answer is a resounding "It depends." If you want to let a sleeping dog lie (or, in this case, a potential train wreck go unattended), then say nothing. It's the other person who seems to have something to say but refuses to open up. It's the other person who's blown a cork. Run for cover. You can't take responsibility for someone else's thoughts and feelings. Right?

Then again, you'll never work through your differences until all parties freely add to the pool of meaning. That means the people who are blowing up or clamming up must participate as well. And while it's true that you can't force others to dialogue, you can take steps to make it safer for them to do so. After all, that's why they've sought the security of silence or violence in the first place. They're afraid that dialogue will make them vulnerable. Somehow they believe that if they engage in real conversation with you, bad things will happen. Your daughter, for instance, believes that if she talks with you, she'll be lectured, grounded, and cut off from the only guy who seems to care about her. Restoring safety is your greatest hope to get your relationship back on track.

EXPLORE OTHERS' PATHS

In Chapter 5 we recommended that whenever you notice safety is at risk, you should step out of the conversation and restore it. When you have offended others through a thoughtless act, apologize. Or if someone has misunderstood your intent, use Contrasting. Explain what you do and don't intend. Finally, if you're simply at odds, find a Mutual Purpose.

Now we add one more skill: *Explore Others' Paths*. Since we've added a model of what's going on inside another person's head (the Path to Action), we now have a whole new tool for helping others feel safe. If we can find a way to let others know that it's okay to share their Path to Action—their facts, and yes, even their nasty stories and ugly feelings—then they'll be more likely to open up.

But what does it take?

Start with Heart—Get Ready to Listen

Be sincere. To get at others' facts and stories, we have to invite them to share what's on their minds. We'll look at how to do this in a minute. For now, let's highlight the point that when you do invite people to share their views, you must mean it. For example, consider the following incident. A patient is exiting a health-care facility. The desk attendant can tell that she is a bit uneasy, maybe even dissatisfied.

"Did everything go all right with the procedure?" the clerk asks.

"Mostly," the patient replies. (If ever there was a hint that something was wrong, the term "mostly" has to be it.)

"Good," the clerk abruptly responds and then follows with a resounding, "Next!"

This is a classic case of pretending to be interested. It falls under the "How are you today?" category of inquiries. Meaning: "Please don't say anything of substance. I'm really just making small talk." When you ask people to open up, be prepared to listen.

Be curious. When you do want to hear from others (and you should because it adds to the pool of meaning), the best way to get at the truth is by making it safe for them to express the stories that are moving them to either silence or violence. This means that at the very moment when most people become furious, we need to become curious. Rather than respond in kind, we need to wonder what's behind the ruckus.

But how? How can we possibly act curious when others are either attacking us or heading for cover? People who routinely seek to find out why others are feeling unsafe have learned that getting at the source of fear and discomfort is the best way to return to dialogue. Either they've seen others do it, or they've stumbled on the formula themselves. In either case, they realize that the cure to silence or violence isn't to respond in kind, but to get at the source. This calls for genuine curiosity—at a time when you're likely to be feeling frustrated or angry.

To help turn your visceral tendency to respond in kind into genuine curiosity, look for opportunities to be curious. Start with a situation where you observe someone becoming emotional and you're still under control—such as a meeting (when you're not personally under attack and are less likely to get hooked). Do your best to get at the person's source of fear or anger. Look for chances to turn on your curiosity rather than kick-start your adrenaline.

To illustrate what can happen as we exercise our curiosity, let's return to our nervous patient.

CLERK: Did everything go all right with the procedure?

PATIENT: Mostly.

CLERK: It sounds like you had a problem of some kind. Is that right?

PATIENT: I'll say. It hurt quite a bit. And besides, isn't the doctor, like, uh, way too old?

In this case, the patient is reluctant to speak up. Perhaps if she shares her honest opinion, she will insult the doctor, or maybe the loyal staff members will become offended. To deal with the problem, the desk attendant lets the patient know that it's safe to talk (as much with his tone as with his words), and she opens up.

Stay curious. When people begin to share their volatile stories and feelings, we now face the risk of pulling out our own Victim, Villain, and Helpless Stories to help us explain why they're saying what they're saying. Unfortunately, since it's rarely fun to hear other people's unflattering stories, we begin to assign negative motives to them for telling the stories. For example:

> CLERK: Well aren't you the ungrateful one! The kind doctor devotes his whole life to helping people and now that he's a little gray around the edges, you want to send him out to pasture!

To avoid overreacting to others' stories, stay curious. Give your brain a problem to stay focused on. Ask: "Why would a reasonable, rational, and decent person say this?" This question keeps you retracing the other person's Path to Action until you see how it all fits together. And in most cases, you end up seeing that under the circumstances, the individual in question drew a fairly reasonable conclusion.

Be patient. When others are acting out their feelings and opinions through silence or violence, it's a good bet they're starting to feel the effects of adrenaline. Even if we do our best to safely and effectively respond to the other person's possible onslaught, we still have to face up to the fact that it's going to take a little while for him or her to settle down. Say, for example, that a friend dumps out an ugly story and you treat it with respect and continue on with the conversation. Even if the two of you now share a similar view, it may seem like your friend is still pushing too hard. While it's natural to move quickly from one *thought* to the next, strong *emotions* take a while to subside. Once the chemicals that fuel emotions are released, they hang around in the bloodstream for a time—in some cases, long after thoughts have changed.

So be patient when exploring how others think and feel. Encourage them to share their path and then wait for their emotions to catch up with the safety that you've created.

Encourage Others to Retrace Their Path

Once you've decided to maintain a curious approach, it's time to help the other person retrace his or her Path to Action. Unfortunately, most of us fail to do so. That's because when others start playing silence or violence games, we're joining the conversation at the *end* of their Path to Action. They've seen and heard things, told themselves a story or two, generated a feeling (possibly a mix of fear and anger or disappointment), and now they're starting to act out their story. That's where we come in. Now, even though we may be hearing their first words, we're coming in somewhere near the end of their path. On the Path to Action model, we're seeing the action at the end of the path—as shown in Figure 8-1.

Every sentence has a history. To get a feel for how complicated and unnerving this process is, remember how you felt the last time your favorite mystery show started late because a football game ran long. As the game wraps up, the screen cross-fades from a trio of announcers to a starlet standing over a murder victim. Along the bottom of the screen are the discomforting words, "We now join this program already in progress."

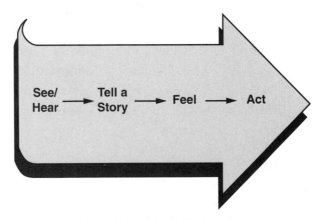

Figure 8-1. The Path to Action

You shake the remote in exasperation. You've missed the entire setup! For the rest of the program you end up guessing about key facts. What happened before you joined in?

Crucial conversations can be equally mysterious and frustrating. When others are in either silence or violence, we're actually joining their Path to Action *already in progress*. Consequently, we've already missed the foundation of the story and we're confused. If we're not careful, we can become defensive. After all, not only are we joining late, but we're also joining at a time when the other person is starting to act offensively.

Break the cycle. And then guess what happens? When we're on the receiving end of someone's retributions, accusations, and cheap shots, rarely do we think: "My, what an interesting story he or she must have told. What do you suppose led to that?" Instead, we match this unhealthy behavior. Our defense mechanisms kick in, and we create our own hasty and ugly Path to Action.

People who know better cut this dangerous cycle by stepping out of the interaction and making it safe for the other person to talk about his or her Path to Action. They perform this feat by encouraging him or her to move away from harsh feelings and knee-jerk reactions and toward the root cause. In essence, they retrace the other person's Path to Action together. At their encouragement, the other person moves from his or her emotions, to what he or she concluded, to what he or she observed.

When we help others retrace their path to its origins, not only do we help curb our reaction, but we also return to the place where the feelings can be resolved—at the source, or the facts and the story behind the emotion.

POWER UP

When? So far we've suggested that when other people appear to have a story to tell and facts to share, it's our job to invite them to do so. Our cues are simple: Others are going to silence or violence. We can see that they're feeling upset, fearful, or angry. We can see that if we don't get at the *source* of their feelings, we'll end up suffering the *effects* of the feelings. These external reactions are our cues to do whatever it takes to help others retrace their Paths to Action.

How? We've also suggested that whatever we do to invite the other person to open up and share his or her path, our invitation must be sincere. As hard as it sounds, we must be sincere in the face of hostility, fear, or even abuse—which leads us to the next question.

What? What are we supposed to actually *do?* What does it take to get others to share their path—stories and facts alike? In a word, it requires *listening*. In order for people to move from acting on their feelings to talking about their conclusions and observations, we must listen in a way that makes it safe for others to share their intimate thoughts. They must believe that when they share their thoughts, they won't offend others or be punished for speaking frankly.

AMPP

To encourage others to share their paths we'll use four power listening tools that can help make it safe for other people to speak frankly. We call the four skills *power* listening tools because they are best remembered with the acronym AMPP—*Ask, Mirror, Paraphrase,* and *Prime.* Luckily, the tools work for both silence and violence games.

Ask to Get Things Rolling

The easiest and most straightforward way to encourage others to share their Path to Action is simply to invite them to express themselves. For example, often all it takes to break an impasse is to seek to understand others' views. When we show genuine interest, people feel less compelled to use silence or violence. For example: "Do you like my new dress, or are you going to call the modesty police?" Wendy smirks.

"What do you mean?" you ask. "I'd like to hear your concerns."

If you're willing to step out of the fray and simply invite the other person to talk about what's really going on, it can go a long way toward breaking the downward spiral and getting to the source of the problem.

Common invitations include:

"What's going on?"
"I'd really like to hear your opinion on this."
"Please let me know if you see it differently."
"Don't worry about hurting my feelings. I really want to hear your thoughts."

Mirror to Confirm Feelings

If asking others to share their path doesn't open things up, mirroring can help build more safety. In mirroring, we take the portion of the other person's Path to Action we have access to and make it safe for him or her to discuss it. All we have so far are actions and some hints about the other person's emotions, so we start there.

When we mirror, as the name suggests, we hold a mirror up to the other person—describing how they look or act. Although we may not understand others' stories or facts, we can see their actions and get clues about their feelings.

This particular tool is most useful when another person's tone of voice or gestures (hints about the emotions behind them) are inconsistent with his or her words. For example: "Don't worry. I'm fine." (But the person in question is saying this with a look that suggests he is actually quite upset. He's frowning, looking around, and sort of kicking at the ground.)

"Really? From the way you're saying that, it doesn't sound like you are."

We explain that while the person may be saying one thing, his or her tone of voice or body posture suggests something else. In doing so, we show respect and concern for him or her.

The most important element of mirroring is our tone of voice. It is not the fact that we are acknowledging others' emotions that creates safety. We create safety when our tone of voice says we're okay with them feeling the way they're feeling. If we do this well, they may conclude that rather than acting out their emotions, they can confidently talk them out with us instead.

So as we describe what we see, we have to do so calmly. If we act upset or as if we're not going to like what others say, we don't build safety. We confirm their suspicions that they need to remain silent.

Examples of mirroring include:

"You say you're okay, but by the tone of your voice, you seem upset."
"You seem angry at me."
"You look nervous about confronting him. Are you sure you're willing to do it?"

Paraphrase to Acknowledge the Story

Asking and mirroring may help you get part of the other person's story out into the open. When you get a clue about *why* the person is feeling as he or she does, you can build additional safety by paraphrasing what you've heard. Be careful not to simply parrot back what was said. Instead, put the message in your own words—usually in an abbreviated form.

"Let's see if I've got this right. You're upset because I've voiced my concern about some of the clothes you wear. And this seems controlling or old-fashioned to you."

The key to paraphrasing, as with mirroring, is to remain calm and collected. Our goal is to make it safe, not to act horrified and suggest that the conversation is about to turn ugly. Stay focused on figuring out how a reasonable, rational, and decent person could have created this Path to Action. This will help you keep from becoming angry or defensive. Simply rephrase what the person has said, and do it in a way that suggests that it's okay, you're trying to understand, and it's safe for him or her to talk candidly.

Don't push too hard. Let's see where we are. We can tell that another person has more to share than he or she is currently sharing. He or she is going to silence or violence, and we want to know why. We want to get back to the source (the facts) where we can solve the problem. To encourage the person to share, we've tried three listening tools. We've asked, mirrored, and paraphrased. The person is still upset, but isn't explaining his or her stories or facts.

Now what? At this point, we may want to back off. After a while, our attempts to make it safe for others can start feeling as if we're pestering or prying. If we push too hard, we violate both purpose and respect. Others may think our purpose is merely to extract what we want from them and conclude that we don't care about them personally. So instead, we back off. Rather than trying to get to the source of the other person's emotions, we either gracefully exit or ask what he or she wants to see happen. Asking people what they want helps them engage their brains in a way that moves to problem solving and away from either attacking or avoiding. It also helps reveal what they think the cause of the problem is.

Prime When You're Getting Nowhere

On the other hand, there are times when you may conclude that others would like to open up but still don't feel safe. Or maybe they're still in violence, haven't come down from the adrenaline, and aren't explaining why they're angry. When this is the case, you might want to try priming. Prime when you believe that the other person still has something to share and might do so with a little more effort on your part.

The power-listening term *priming* comes from the expression "priming the pump." If you've ever worked an old-fashioned hand pump, you understand the metaphor. With a pump, you often have to pour some water into it to get it running. Then it works just fine. When it comes to power listening, sometimes you have to offer your best guess at what the other person is thinking or feeling. You have to pour some meaning into the pool before the other person will do the same.

A few years back, one of the authors was working with an executive team that had decided to add an afternoon shift to one of the company's work areas. The machinery wasn't being fully utilized, and the company couldn't afford to keep the area open without adding a three-to-midnight crew. This, of course, meant that the people currently working days would now have to rotate every two weeks to afternoons. It was a tortured but necessary choice.

As the execs held a meeting to announce the unpopular change, the existing work crew went silent. They were obviously unhappy, but nobody would say anything. The operations manager was afraid that people would misinterpret the company's actions as nothing more than a grab for more money. In truth, the area was losing money, but the decision was made with the current employees in mind. With no second shift, there would be no jobs. He also knew that asking people to rotate shifts and to be away from loved ones during the afternoon and evening would cause horrible burdens.

As people sat silently fuming, the executive did his best to get them to talk so that they wouldn't walk away with unresolved feelings. He mirrored, "I can see you're upset—who wouldn't be? Is there anything we can do?" Nothing. Finally, he primed. That is, he took his best guess at what they might be thinking, said it in a way that showed it was okay to talk about it, and then went on from there. "Are you thinking that the only reason we're doing this is to make money? That maybe we don't care about your personal lives?"

After a brief pause, someone answered: "Well, it sure looks like that. Do you have any idea how much trouble this is going to cause?" Then someone else chimed in and the discussion was off and running.

Now, this is not the kind of thing you would do unless nothing else has worked. You really want to hear from others, and you have a very strong idea of what they're probably thinking. Priming is an act of good faith, taking risks, becoming vulnerable, and building safety in hopes that others will share their meaning.

But What If They're Wrong?

Sometimes it feels dangerous to sincerely explore the views of someone whose path is wildly different from your own. He or she could be completely wrong, and we're acting calm and collected. This makes us nervous.

To keep ourselves from feeling nervous while exploring others' paths—no matter how different or wrong they seem—remember we're trying to understand their point of view, not necessarily agree with it or support it. Understanding doesn't equate with agreement. By coming to understand another person's Path to Action, we are not accepting it as absolute truth. There will be plenty of time later for us to share our path as well. For now, we're merely trying to get at what others think in order to understand why they're feeling the way they're feeling and doing what they're doing.

EXPLORING WENDY'S PATH

Now let's put the several skills together in a single interaction. We'll return to Wendy. She has just come home from a date with the guy who has you frightened. You yank the door open, pull Wendy into the house, and double-bolt your entrance. Then you talk, sort of.

> WENDY: How could you embarrass me like that! I get one boy to like me, and now he'll never talk to me again! I hate you!
>
> YOU: That wasn't a boy. That was a future inmate. You're worth more than that. Why are you wasting your time with him?
>
> WENDY: You're ruining my life. Leave me alone!

After Wendy's bedroom door slams shut, you drop down into a chair in the living room. Your emotions are running wild. You're terrified about what could happen if Wendy continues to see this guy. You're hurt that she said she hated you. You feel that your relationship with her is spiraling out of control.

So you ask yourself, "What do I really want?" As you mull this question over, your motives change. The goals of controlling Wendy and defending your pride drop from the top to the bottom of your list. The goal that's now at the top looks a bit more inspiring: "I want to understand what she's feeling. I want a good relationship with Wendy. And I want her to make choices that will make her happy."

You're not sure if tonight is the best or worst time to talk, but you know that talking is the only path forward. So you give it a shot.

> YOU: (*Tapping on door.*) Wendy? May I talk with you please?
>
> WENDY: Whatever.

(You enter her room and sit on her bed.)

YOU: I'm really sorry for embarrassing you like that. That was a bad way to handle it. [*Apologize to build safety*]

WENDY: It's just that you do that a lot. It's like you want to control everything in my life.

YOU: Can we talk about that? [*Ask*]

WENDY: (*Sounding angry*) It's no big deal. You're the parent, right?

YOU: From the way you say that, it sounds like it is a big deal. [*Mirror*] I really would like to hear what makes you think I'm trying to control your life. [*Ask*]

WENDY: What, so you can tell me more ways that I'm screwed up? I've finally got one friend who accepts me, and you're trying to chase him away!

YOU: So you feel like I don't approve of you, and your friend is one person who does? [*Paraphrase*]

WENDY: It's not just you. All my friends have lots of boys who like them. Doug's the first guy who's even called me. I don't know—never mind.

YOU: I can see how you'd feel badly when others are getting attention from boys and you aren't. I'd probably feel the same way. [*Paraphrase*]

WENDY: Then how could you embarrass me like that?!

YOU: Honey, I'd like to take a stab at something here. I wonder if part of the reason you've started dressing differently and hanging out with different friends is because you're not feeling cared about and valued by boys, by your parents, and by others right now. Is that part of it? [*Prime*]

WENDY: (*Sits quietly for a long time*) Why am I so ugly? I really work on how I look but . . .

From here, the conversation goes to the real issues, parent and daughter discuss what's really going on, and both come to a better understanding of each other.

REMEMBER YOUR ABCs

Let's say you did your level best to make it safe for the other person to talk. After asking, mirroring, paraphrasing, and eventually priming, the other person opened up and shared his or her path. It's now your turn to talk. But what if you disagree? Some of the other person's facts are wrong, and his or her stories are completely fouled up. Well, at least they're a lot different from the story you've been telling. Now what?

Agree

As you watch families and work groups take part in heated debates, it's common to notice a rather intriguing phenomenon. Although the various parties you're observing are violently arguing, in truth, they're in *violent agreement*. They actually agree on every important point, but they're still fighting. They've found a way to turn subtle differences into a raging debate.

For example, last night your teenage son broke his curfew again. You and your spouse have spent the morning arguing about the infraction. Last time James came in late, you agreed to ground him, but today you're upset because it seems like your spouse is backpedaling by suggesting that James still be able to attend a football camp this week. Turns out it was just a misunderstanding. You and your spouse *agree* to the grounding—the central issue. You thought your spouse was reneging on the agreement when, in truth, you just hadn't actually resolved the date the grounding would start. You had to step back and listen to what you were both saying to realize that you weren't really disagreeing, but violently agreeing.

Most arguments consist of battles over the 5 to 10 percent of the facts and stories that people disagree over. And while it's true that people eventually need to work through differences, you shouldn't start there. Start with an area of agreement.

So here's the take-away. If you completely agree with the other person's path, say so and move on. Agree when you agree. Don't turn an agreement into an argument.

Build

Of course, the reason most of us turn agreements into debates is because we disagree with a certain portion of what the other person has said. Never mind that it's a *minor* portion. If it's a point of disagreement, we'll jump all over it like a fleeing criminal.

Actually, we're trained to look for minor errors from an early age. For instance, we learn in kindergarten that if you have the right answer, you're the teacher's pet. Being right is good. Of course, if others have the right answer they get to be the pet. So being right first is even better. You learn to look for even the tiniest of errors in others' facts, thinking, or logic. Then you point out the errors. Being right at the expense of others is best.

By the time you finish your education, you have a virtual Ph.D. in catching trivial differences and turning them into a major deal. So when another person offers up a suggestion (based on facts and stories), you're looking to disagree. And when you do find a minor difference, you turn this snack into a meal. Instead of remaining in healthy dialogue, you end up in violent agreement.

On the other hand, when you watch people who are skilled in dialogue, it becomes clear that they're not playing this everyday game of Trivial Pursuit—looking for trivial differences and then proclaiming them aloud. In fact, they're looking for points of agreement. As a result, they'll often start with the words "I agree." Then they talk about the part they agree with. At least, that's where they start.

Now when the other person has merely *left out an element* of the argument, skilled people will agree and then build. Rather than saying: "Wrong. You forgot to mention . . .," they say: "Absolutely. In addition, I noticed that . . ."

If you agree with what has been said but the information is incomplete, build. Point out areas of agreement and then add elements that were left out of the discussion.

Compare

Finally, if you do disagree, compare your path with the other person's. That is, rather than suggesting that *he* or *she* is wrong, suggest that you differ. He or she may, in fact, be wrong, but you don't know for sure until you hear both sides of the story. For now, you just know that the two of you differ. So instead of pronouncing "Wrong!" start with a tentative but candid opening such as "I think I see things differently. Let me describe how."

Then share your path using the STATE skills from Chapter 7. That is, begin by sharing your observations. Share them tentatively, and invite others to test your ideas. After you've shared your path, invite the other person to help you compare it with his or her experience. Work together to explore and explain the differences.

In summary, to help remember these skills, think of your ABCs. *Agree* when you agree. *Build* when others leave out key pieces. *Compare* when you differ. Don't turn differences into debates that lead to unhealthy relationships and bad results.

SUMMARY—EXPLORE OTHERS' PATHS

To encourage the free flow of meaning and help others leave silence or violence behind, explore their Paths to Action. Start with an attitude of curiosity and patience. This helps restore safety.

Then, use four powerful listening skills to retrace the other person's Path to Action to its origins.

- _Ask_. Start by simply expressing interest in the other person's views.

- _Mirror_. Increase safety by respectfully acknowledging the emotions people appear to be feeling.

- _Paraphrase_. As others begin to share part of their story, restate what you've heard to show not just that you understand, but also that it's safe for them to share what they're thinking.

- _Prime_. If others continue to hold back, prime. Take your best guess at what they may be thinking and feeling.

As you begin to share your views, remember:

- _Agree_. Agree when you do.

- _Build_. If others leave something out, agree where you do, then build.

- _Compare_. When you do differ significantly, don't suggest others are wrong. Compare your two views.

9

Move to Action

How to Turn Crucial Conversations into Action and Results

Up until this point we've suggested that getting more meaning into the pool helps with dialogue. It's the *one thing* that helps people make savvy decisions that, in turn, lead to smart actions. In order to encourage this free flow of meaning, we've shared the skills we've been able to learn by watching people who are gifted at dialogue. By now, if you've followed some or all of this advice, you're walking around with full pools. People who walk near you should hear the sloshing.

It's time we add two final skills. Having more meaning in the pool, even jointly owning it, doesn't guarantee that we all agree on what we're going to do with the meaning. For example, when teams or families meet and generate a host of ideas, they often fail to convert the ideas into action for two reasons:

- They have unclear expectations about how decisions will be made.

- They do a poor job of acting on the decisions they do make.

This can be dangerous. In fact, when people move from adding meaning to the pool to moving to action, it's a prime time for new challenges to arise. Who is supposed to take the assignment? That can be controversial. How are we supposed to decide in the first place? That can be emotional. Let's take a look at what it takes to solve each of these problems. First, making decisions.

DIALOGUE IS NOT DECISION MAKING

The two riskiest times in crucial conversations tend to be at the beginning and at the end. The beginning is risky because you have to find a way to create safety or else things go awry. The end is dicey because if you aren't careful about how you clarify the conclusion and decisions flowing from your Pool of Shared Meaning, you can run into violated expectations later on. This can happen in two ways.

How are decisions going to be made? First, people may not understand how decisions are going to be made. For example, Cara is miffed. Rene just plunked down a brochure for a three-day cruise and announced he had made reservations and even paid the five hundred dollar deposit for an outside suite.

A week ago they had a crucial conversation about vacation plans. Both expressed their views and preferences respectfully and candidly. It wasn't easy, but at the end they concluded a cruise suited both quite well. And yet Cara is miffed, and Rene is stunned that Cara is anything less than ecstatic.

Cara agreed *in principle* about a cruise. She didn't agree with this particular cruise. Rene thought that any cruise would be fine and made a decision on his own. Have fun on the cruise, Rene.

Are we ever going to decide? The second problem with decision making occurs when no decision gets made. Either ideas slip away and dissipate, or people can't figure out what to do with them. Or maybe everyone is waiting for everyone else to make the decisions. "Hey, we filled the pool. Now you do something with it." In any case, decisions drag on forever.

DECIDE HOW TO DECIDE

Both of these problems are solved if, before making a decision, the people involved decide how to decide. Don't allow people to assume that dialogue is decision making. Dialogue is a process for getting all relevant meaning into a shared pool. That process, of course, involves everyone. However, simply because everyone is allowed to share their meaning—actually encouraged to share their meaning—doesn't mean they are then guaranteed to take part in making all the decisions. To avoid violated expectations, separate dialogue from decision making. Make it clear how decisions will be made—who will be involved and why.

When the line of authority is clear. When you're in a position of authority, you decide which method of decision making you'll use. Managers and parents, for example, decide how to decide. It's part of their responsibility as leaders. For instance, VPs don't ask hourly employees to decide on pricing changes or product lines. That's the leaders' job. Parents don't ask small children to pick their home security device or to set their own curfew. That's the job of the parent. Of course, both leaders and parents turn more decisions over to their direct reports and children when they warrant the responsibility, but it's still the authority figure who decides what method of decision making to employ. Deciding what decisions to turn over and when to do it is part of their stewardship.

When the line of authority isn't clear. When there is no clear line of authority, deciding how to decide can be quite difficult.

For instance, consider a conversation we referred to earlier—the one you had with your daughter's schoolteacher. Should you hold your child back? Whose choice is this anyway? Who decides whose choice it is? Does everyone have a say, then a vote? Is it the school officials' responsibility, so they choose? Since parents have ultimate responsibility, should they consult with the appropriate experts and then decide? Is there even a clear answer to this tough question?

A case like this is hand-tooled for dialogue. All of the participants need to get their meaning into the pool—including their opinions about who should make the final choice. That's part of the meaning you need to discuss. If you don't openly talk about who decides and why, and your opinions vary widely, you're likely to end up in a heated battle that can only be resolved in court. Handled poorly, that's exactly where these kind of issues are resolved—*The Jones Family vs. Happy Valley School District.*

So what's a person to do? Talk openly about your child's abilities and interests *as well as* about how the final choice will be made. Don't mention lawyers or a lawsuit in your opening comments; this only reduces safety and sets up an adversarial climate. Your goal is to have an open, honest, and healthy discussion about a child, not to exert your influence, make threats, or somehow beat the educators. Stick with the opinions of the experts at hand, and discuss how and why they should be involved. When decision-making authority is unclear, use your best dialogue skills to get meaning into the pool. Jointly decide how to decide.

The Four Methods of Decision Making

When you're deciding how to decide, it helps to have a way of talking about the decision-making options available. There are four common ways of making decisions: command, consult, vote, and consensus. These four options represent increasing degrees of involvement. Increased involvement, of course, brings the benefit of increased commitment along with the curse of decreased decision-making efficiency. Savvy people choose from among these four methods of decision making the one that best suits their particular circumstances.

Command

Let's start with decisions that are made with no involvement whatsoever. This happens in one of two ways. Either outside forces place demands on us (demands that leave us no wiggle room), or we turn decisions over to others and then follow their lead. We don't care enough to be involved—let someone else do the work.

In the case of external forces, customers set prices, agencies mandate safety standards, and other governing bodies simply hand us demands. As much as employees like to think their bosses are sitting around making choices, for the most part they're simply passing on the demands of the circumstances. These are command decisions. With command decisions, it's not our job to decide what to do. It's our job to decide how to make it work.

In the case of turning decisions over to others, we decide either that this is such a low-stakes issue that we don't care enough to take part or that we completely trust the ability of the delegate to make the right decision. More involvement adds nothing. In strong teams and great relationships, many decisions are made by turning the final choice over to someone we trust to make a good decision. We don't want to take the time ourselves and gladly turn the decision over to others.

Consult

Consulting is a process whereby decision makers invite others to influence them before they make their choice. You can consult with experts, a representative population, or even everyone who wants to offer an opinion. Consulting can be an efficient way of gaining ideas and support without bogging down the decision-making process. At least not too much. Wise leaders, parents, and even couples frequently make decisions in this way. They gather ideas, evaluate options, make a choice, and then inform the broader population.

Vote

Voting is best suited to situations where efficiency is the highest value—and you're selecting from a number of good options. Members of the team realize they may not get their first choice, but frankly they don't want to waste time talking the issue to death. They may discuss options for a while and then call for a vote. When facing several decent options, voting is a great time saver but should never be used when team members don't agree to support whatever decision is made. In these cases, consensus is required.

Consensus

This method can be both a great blessing and a frustrating curse. Consensus means you talk until everyone honestly agrees to one decision. This method can produce tremendous unity and high-quality decisions. If misapplied, it can also be a horrible waste of time. It should only be used with (1) high-stakes and complex issues or (2) issues where everyone absolutely must support the final choice.

HOW TO CHOOSE

Now that we know the four methods, let's explore which method to use at which time—along with some hints about how to avoid common blunders.

Four Important Questions

When choosing among the four methods of decision making, consider the following questions.

1. *Who cares?* Determine who genuinely wants to be involved in the decision along with those who will be affected. These are your candidates for involvement. Don't involve people who don't care.

2. *Who knows?* Identify who has the expertise you need to make the best decision. Encourage these people to take part. Try not to involve people who contribute no new information.

3. *Who must agree?* Think of those whose cooperation you might need in the form of authority or influence in any decisions you might make. It's better to involve these people than to surprise them and then suffer their open resistance.

4. *How many people is it worth involving?* Your goal should be to involve the fewest number of people while still considering the quality of the decision along with the support that people will give it. Ask: "Do we have enough people to make a good choice? Will others have to be involved to gain their commitment?"

How about you? Here's a suggestion for a great exercise for teams or couples, particularly those that are frustrated about decision making. Make a list of some of the important decisions made in the team or relationship. Then discuss how each decision is currently made, and how each *should* be made—using the four important questions. After discussing each decision, decide how you will make decisions in the future. A crucial conversation about your decision-making practices can resolve many frustrating issues.

DECISION-MAKING BLUNDERS AND SOLUTIONS

Now, let's look at each of the four methods in turn. What are the common blunders associated with each, and more importantly, how can we avoid them?

Appropriate Use of Command

The mistake. For years, employees have complained that their bosses are far too bossy. They hand out orders like Halloween candy. They not only tell people what to do, but also restrict them to only one way of doing it. They give directions down to the tiniest detail when it would be better to allow the employee to work out the details of how the job will be done. After all, the employee is not only closest to the job, but is also the expert on how to do it.

Today's generation of employees (and children, for that matter) expects to be involved in more decisions than their grandparents ever faced. That's where the empowerment movement came from. Younger people don't see themselves as a pair of hands seeking direction. They want to think. They want to decide. They're willing to take on more responsibility.

So as you face a potential "command decision," consider the following:

- *Don't pass out orders like candy.* We face enough command decisions (constraints placed on us by outside forces) without making up new ones. As a general rule, if people can make choices, allow them to do so. Don't tie their hands without reason. With kids, for example, you may establish rules about cleanliness in the common areas of the home, but you may let them choose (within the boundaries of hygiene) how to keep their rooms.

- *When you face a command decision, ask which elements are flexible.* Once a standard has been set by an agency or an order placed by a customer, while you may not be able to decide what to work on or what standards to follow, you can decide *how* to work. Find out where you do have degrees of freedom and then allow others to choose within these boundaries.

- *Explain why.* When handing down an order, explain the reason behind the demand. Knowing *why* helps make *what* a lot easier. For example, if you decide overtime is needed to meet a deadline, it helps to explain why you came to this conclusion.

The Dos and Don'ts of Consultation

The most obvious problem with consultation is that people believe that if you involve them in sharing ideas, they get to make the decision. It's easy to see how this happens since *you* ask for people's input, *you* weigh all the options, and *you* make a decision. Then two-thirds of those you asked feel violated because you didn't do what they told you to do.

Dialogue is a great tool for consultation. It enables you to get all meaning into the shared pool. But before people start contributing, be sure they understand that the fact that you are consulting with them does not mean that eventually the decision will be made by consensus.

When should you use consultation? Consult when (1) many people will be affected, (2) you can gather information relatively easily, (3) people care about the decision, and (4) there are many options, some of them controversial.

When these conditions apply, find a way to touch base with a lot of people in different positions, locations, and functions before moving on. Don't simply call on your friends and buddies. Also, consider the following:

- *Don't pretend to consult.* If you've already made up your mind, don't go through the charade of involving people, only to do what you wanted to do all along. For example, the boss calls on people and then strikes down ideas that aren't in line with what he or she has in mind, while giving subtle clues and gentle rewards to those who stumble onto the "right idea."

- *Announce what you're doing.* When you are only going to involve a sample of the people who will be affected, let others know who these people are so they can talk to them if they like. This is akin to holding neighborhood political meetings. Not everyone will show up, but people who want to take part can take part.

- *Report your decision.* When others are kind enough to share their opinions (whether you take their advice or not), they deserve to know what you decide and why. Don't try to keep your decision a secret because you're afraid you'll offend people. They'll soon learn of the decision anyway. Better to hear it from you and not through the grapevine.

Holding a Good Vote

- *Weigh the consequences.* Voting by its very nature creates winners and losers. So you have to be careful. You should only take a vote when you know that the losers don't really care all that much. Otherwise you may be fighting the battle for a long time after the decision has been made. With children, for example, have them carefully consider if they're okay with losing before they agree to have you take a poll.

- *Know when to vote.* When matters aren't all that weighty, there are many good choices to select from, and people care about not taking too much time, then take a vote. It's the kind of thing you do to reduce lengthy lists. Vote to reduce the list of twenty items to five. Then use consensus to select from the five.

- *Don't cop out with a vote.* When everyone cares a great deal about an issue and people are having trouble coming to a choice, don't stop and call for a vote. Votes should never replace patient analysis and healthy dialogue. If you find yourself saying, "All right, we'll never agree so let's vote," you're copping out.

Surviving the Joys of Consensus

Imagine you're working with six people, all housed in a tight space. Things are sailing along smoothly until one day when a new employee shows up with a huge boom box—it looks like a storage shed with a handle on top. It has its own set of wheels. Thirty seconds later, the pulsing sounds of a band called Decibel Death fill your area. You're not happy. You fear your head will explode. How might you handle this?

Or how about this challenge? How do you decide the temperature of the room you share?

Or how about this one? Where does the entire family go on vacation?

Or if you want to take on a real corker—who performs the most distasteful jobs at home and at work?

These are the kinds of decisions where neither consultation nor command tools work very well. Everyone is affected, everyone cares, and there are several options—not equally liked. This kind of crucial conversation calls for consensus. Everyone meets, honestly and openly discusses the choices, comes up with a variety of ideas, and jointly makes a decision that each person agrees to support. As is the case with all crucial conversations, this is not an easy process and is routinely handled poorly. Here are some hints for avoiding common mistakes.

- *Don't force consensus onto everything.* As Abraham Maslow once said, "If the only tool you have is a hammer, you tend to see every problem as a nail." Consensus decision making is one of today's widely used hammers. People apply it to situations that don't deserve the time and attention needed to come to a consensus or that can't be solved unanimously.

For example, forty people are brought together to decide on the color of the work area. That's too many people. Use consultation. A team meets to decide if each team member should use a certain type of coffee mug (we're not making this up). Let people choose their own. A couple asks their son to decide his own punishment. Not always a good idea. Some decisions need to be made by command.

- *Don't pretend that everyone gets his or her first choice.* Nobody ever said that with consensus everyone gets his or her way. Consensus isn't about getting your way; it's about doing what's best for the family or team. It requires give and take. It demands compromise followed by the resolve to support (in some cases) your second or third choice—because it's best for the group.

- *No martyrs please.* Healthy teams and families are good at coming to consensus because they're good at dialogue. They don't toggle from silence to violence or otherwise play games in order to get their way. Since everyone has a say and says it well, healthy groups don't end up with the same people constantly giving in and then playing the role of martyr. "Are you enjoying the theme park? Don't worry about me. I'll just sit here on the curb and try to think of what it would have been like to go to Paris."

- *Don't take turns.* Decisions should be based on merit, not on who offers up the options. Don't take turns getting your way. "Well, Leona, my recollection is that you gave in last time, so I guess it's our turn to roll over on this one." Make the decision based on which proposal best meets the needs of the group. This doesn't mean that people don't take into account personalities or strength of desire (deferring to those who care a great deal when you don't care all that much, for instance). It simply means that the future of your family or organization shouldn't come down to the flip of a coin.

- *Don't engage in postdecision lobbying.* Consensus decisions should be made out in the open and as an entire group. Withholding your reservations and then approaching individuals after the discussion is both inefficient and disloyal. If you have an issue, bring it up in front of the group. Leave unhealthy alliances, dirty deals, and secret discussions to people who are on reality game shows. They can afford to abuse one another, take their winnings, and then go their separate ways. With families and work groups, you stay together long after the ugly behavior and you suffer the long-term consequences.

- *Don't say "I told you so."* Nothing is quite so annoying as having someone agree on a choice (his or her second choice, perhaps) and then cry, "I told you so!" when it doesn't work out. Once you've decided on something as a group, support the idea—not *even* when it fails, but *particularly* when it fails. There's no room for fair-weather family members or teammates. Show character. When an idea doesn't work out, own the failure together.

Advice for the Time-Bound

There are times when you know you should involve others in a decision, but you absolutely have to make a decision by a certain time. In these cases, consider selecting a fallback decision-making plan.

For example, you could announce: "We have a critical decision to make that affects all of us, and it must be made by ten sharp. I propose that we use consensus to decide. However, if by 9:45 we have not come to consensus, then it will become a consult decision. I will use your input, and I will decide."

This strategy allows you to try for the optimum decision-making method, but it leaves you a back door without making you look like a despot when time runs out.

MAKING ASSIGNMENTS—PUTTING DECISIONS INTO ACTION

Now let's take a look at the final step. You've engaged in healthy dialogue, filled the pool of meaning, decided how you're going to draw from the pool, and eventually come to some decisions. It's time to do something. Some of the items may have been completely resolved during the discussion, but many may require a person or team to do something. You'll have to make assignments.

As you might suspect, when you're involved with two or more people, there's a chance that there will be some confusion. To avoid common traps, make sure you consider the following four elements:

- Who?
- Does what?
- By when?
- How will you follow up?

Who?

To quote an English proverb, "Everybody's business is nobody's business." If you don't make an actual assignment to an actual person, there's a good chance that nothing will ever come of all the work you've gone through to make a decision.

When it's time to pass out assignments, remember, there is no "we." "We," when it comes to assignments, actually means, "not me." It's code. Even when individuals are not trying to duck an assignment, the term "we" can lead them to believe that others are taking on the responsibility.

Assign a name to every responsibility. This especially applies at home. If you're divvying up household chores, be sure you've got a specific person to go with each chore. That is, if you assign two or three people to take on a task, appoint one of them the responsible party. Otherwise, any sense of responsibility will be lost in a flurry of finger-pointing later on.

Does What?

Be sure to spell out the exact deliverables you have in mind. The fuzzier the expectations, the higher the likelihood of disappointment. For example, the eccentric entrepreneur Howard Hughes once assigned a team of engineers to design and build the world's first steam-powered car. When sharing his dream of a vehicle that could run on heated water, he gave them virtually no direction.

After several years of intense labor the engineers successfully produced the first prototype by running dozens of pipes through the car's body—thus solving the problem of where to put all the water required to run a steam-powered car. The vehicle was essentially a giant radiator.

When Hughes asked the engineers what would happen if the car got into a wreck, they nervously explained that the passengers would be boiled alive, much like lobsters in a pot. Hughes was so upset in what the crew came up with that he insisted they cut it up into pieces no larger than three inches. That was the end of the project.

Learn from Hughes. When you're first agreeing on an assignment, clarify up front the exact details of what you want.

Couples get into trouble in this area when one of the parties doesn't want to take the time to think carefully about the "deliverables" and then later on becomes upset because his or her unstated desires weren't met. Have you ever remodeled a room with a loved one? Then you know what we're talking about. Better to spend the time up front clarifying exactly what you want rather than waste resources and hurt feelings on the back end.

To help clarify deliverables, use Contrasting. If you've seen people misunderstand an assignment in the past, explain the common mistake as an example of what you *don't* want. If possible, point to physical examples. Rather than talk in the abstract, bring a prototype or sample. We learned this particular trick when hiring a set designer. The renowned designer talked about what he would deliver, and it sounded great to us. Twenty-five thousand dollars later he delivered something that would never work. We had to start over from scratch. From that day on we've learned to point to pictures and talk about what we want and don't want. The clearer the picture of the deliverable, the less likely you'll be unpleasantly surprised.

By When?

It's shocking how often people leave this element out of an assignment. Instead of giving a deadline, people simply point to the setting sun of "someday." With vague or unspoken deadlines, other urgencies come up, and the assignment finds its way to the bottom of the pile, where it is soon forgotten. Assignments without deadlines are far better at producing guilt than stimulating action. Goals without deadlines aren't goals; they're merely directions.

How Will You Follow Up?

Always agree on how often and by what method you'll follow up on the assignment. It could be a simple email confirming the completion of a project. It might be a full report in a team or family meeting. More often than not, it comes down to progress checks along the way.

It's actually fairly easy to build follow-up methods into the assignment. For example: "Call me on my cell phone when you finish your homework. Then you can go play with friends. Okay?"

Or perhaps you'll prefer to rely on milestones: "Let me know when you've completed your library research. Then we'll sit down and look at the next steps." Milestones, of course, must be linked to a drop-dead date. "Let me know as soon you've completed the research component of this project. You've got until the last week in November, but if you finish earlier, give me a call."

Remember, if you want people to feel accountable, you must give them an opportunity to account. Build an expectation for follow-up into every assignment.

DOCUMENT YOUR WORK

Once again, a proverb comes to mind. "One dull pencil is worth six sharp minds." Don't leave your hard work to memory. If you've gone to the effort to complete a crucial conversation, don't fritter away all the meaning you created by trusting your memories. Write down the details of conclusions, decisions, and assignments. Remember to record who does what by when. Revisit your notes at key times (usually the next meeting) and review assignments.

As you review what was supposed to be completed, hold people accountable. When someone fails to deliver on a promise, it's time for dialogue. Discuss the issue by using the STATE skills we covered in Chapter 7. By holding people accountable, not only do you increase their motivation and ability to deliver on promises, but you create a culture of integrity.

SUMMARY—MOVE TO ACTION

Turn your successful crucial conversations into great decisions and united action by avoiding the two traps of violated expectations and inaction.

Decide How to Decide

- *Command.* Decisions are made without involving others.
- *Consult.* Input is gathered from the group and then a subset decides.
- *Vote.* An agreed-upon percentage swings the decision.
- *Consensus.* Everyone comes to an agreement and then supports the final decision.

Finish Clearly

Determine *who* does *what* by *when*. Make the deliverables crystal clear. Set a *follow-up* time. Record the commitments and then follow up. Finally, hold people accountable to their promises.

10

Communication works for those who work at it.

—JOHN POWELL

Putting It All Together

Tools for Preparing and Learning

If you read the previous pages in a short period of time, you probably feel like an anaconda who just swallowed a warthog. It's a lot to digest.

You may well be wondering at this point how you can possibly keep all these ideas straight—especially during something as unpredictable and fast moving as a crucial conversation.

This chapter will help with the daunting task of making dialogue tools and skills memorable and useable. First, we'll simplify things by sharing what we've heard from people who have changed their lives by using these skills. Second, we'll lay out a model that can help you visually organize the seven dialogue principles. Third, we'll walk through an example of a crucial conversation where all the dialogue principles are applied.

TWO LEVERS

Over the years, people often tell us that the principles and skills contained in this book have helped them a great deal. But how? In what way can the printed word lead to important changes?

After watching people at home and at work, as well as interviewing them, we've learned that most people make progress not by focusing on specific skills—at least to start with—but instead by applying two of the main principles in this book. We hope that as we share their success strategies with you, you'll feel more confident getting started on the road to improved results and relationships.

Learn to Look. The first lever for positive change is Learn to Look. That is, people who improve their dialogue skills continually ask themselves whether they're in or out of dialogue. This alone makes a huge difference. Even people who can't remember or never learned the skills of STATE or CRIB, etc., are able to benefit from this material by simply asking if they're falling into silence or violence. They may not know exactly how to fix the specific problem they're facing, but they do know that if they're not in dialogue, it can't be good. And then they try something to get back to dialogue. As it turns out, trying something is better than doing nothing.

So remember to ask the following important question: "Are we playing games or are we in dialogue?" It's a wonderful start.

Many people get additional help in learning to look from their friends. They go through training as families or teams. As they share concepts and ideas, they learn a common vocabulary. This shared way of talking about crucial conversations helps people change.

Perhaps the most common way that the language of dialogue finds itself into everyday conversation is with the expression, "I think we've moved away from dialogue." This simple reminder helps people catch themselves early on, before the damage is severe. As we've watched executive teams, work groups, and couples simply go public with the fact that they're starting to move toward silence or violence, others often recognize the problem and take corrective action. "You're right. I'm not telling you what needs to be said," or "I'm sorry. I have been trying to force my ideas on you."

Make It Safe. The second lever is Make It Safe. We've suggested that dialogue consists of the free flow of meaning and that the number one flow stopper is a lack of safety. When you notice that you and others have moved away from dialogue, do something to make it safer. Anything. We've suggested a few skills, but those are merely a handful of common practices. They're not immutable principles. To no one's surprise, there many things you can do to increase safety. If you simply realize that your challenge is to make it safer, nine out of ten times you'll intuitively do something that helps.

Sometimes you'll build safety by asking a question and showing interest in others' views. Sometimes an appropriate touch (with loved ones and family members—not at work where touching can equate with harassment) can communicate safety. Apologies, smiles, even a request for a brief "time out" can help restore safety when things get dicey. The main idea is to make it safe. Do something to make others comfortable. And remember, virtually every skill we've covered in this book, from Contrasting to CRIB, offers a tool for building safety.

These two levers form the basis for recognizing, building, and maintaining dialogue. When the concept of dialogue is introduced, these are the ideas most people can readily take in and apply to crucial conversations. Now let's move on to a discussion of the rest of the principles we've covered.

A MODEL OF DIALOGUE

To help organize our thinking and to make it easier to recall the principles (and when to apply them), let's look at the model shown in Figure 10-1. It begins with concentric circles—like a target. Notice that the center circle is the Pool of Shared Meaning—it's the center of the target, or the aim of dialogue. When meaning flows freely, it finds its way into this pool, which represents people's best collective thinking.

Surrounding the Pool of Shared Meaning is safety. Safety allows us to share meaning and keeps us from moving into silence or violence. When conversations become crucial, safety must be strong.

Watch for games. Next you'll notice that we've portrayed the behaviors to watch when thinking about safety. These are the six silence and violence behaviors we look for in others and in out-

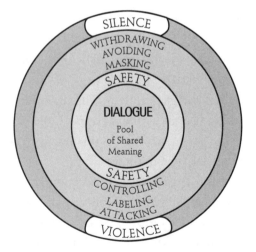

Figure 10-1. The Dialogue Model

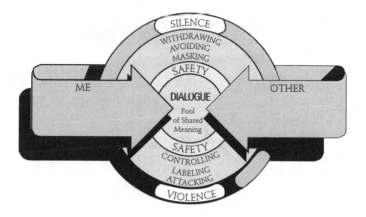

Figure 10-2. The Dialogue Model

breaks of our own Style Under Stress. When we see these or similar behaviors, we know that safety is weak. This is a cue to step out of the content of the conversation, strengthen safety, and then step back in. Remember, don't back away or weaken the argument. Just rebuild safety. Do it quickly. The further you move from dialogue into silence or violence, the harder it is to get back and the greater the costs.

Now, let's add people to our model.

Me and Others. (Figure 10-2). You are the "ME" arrow on the model. Others are included in the "OTHER" arrow. The arrows (both pointed to the center of the pool) show that both we and others are in dialogue. All our meaning is flowing freely into the shared pool. Learn to Look means we watch for when either of these two arrows begins to point upward or downward, toward silence or violence. When this happens, either you or others are starting to play games.

Watching and building conditions. (Figure 10-3). When you see yourself drifting to silence or violence, Start with Heart. Keep

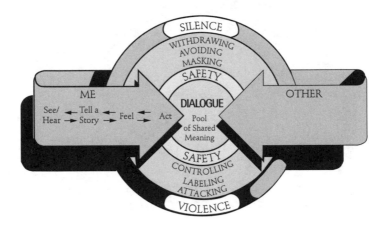

Figure 10-3. The Dialogue Model

yourself in dialogue by focusing on what you really want and then behaving as if you really do want it. Avoid the Sucker's Choices that make it appear as if silence and violence are the only options.

When your emotions start running strong and taking control of the conversation, use the Master My Stories principle to bring your arrow back to the Pool of Shared Meaning. Retrace your Path to Action, watch for clever stories, and tell the rest of the story.

When others move to silence or violence, Make It Safe. As we strengthen safety, others are more likely to lay aside their silence and violence and move back toward dialogue in the center.

What to do. The next three principles teach us what to do with our meaning. First, we learned to STATE My Path. We share our own sensitive or controversial views by following our Path to Action. We share the facts first and then tentatively share our story. We then demonstrate we're serious about dialogue by encouraging others to share their story (Figure 10-4)—especially if it's different from our own.

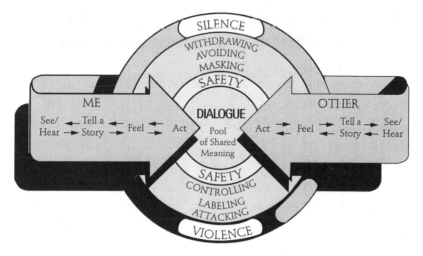

Figure 10-4. The Dialogue Model

To help others share their meaning, we Explore Others' Paths. We ask, mirror, paraphrase, and prime (AMPP) as needed to get to their feelings, stories, and facts. As we use these skills effectively, we demonstrate that their concerns are *discussable*—that dialogue can actually work. This helps others feel safer surrendering their silence and violence and joining us in dialogue.

Finally, with the Pool of Shared Meaning full, we Move to Action. We ensure that we are clear about how decisions are being made and about what the decisions are. And we follow up to ensure that dialogue leads to positive actions and results.

You can use the Dialogue Model first to diagnose what's going on. Remember to ask: "Where am I?" "Where are others?" "Are we in dialogue or in some form of silence or violence?"

Next ask, "Where do I want to be?" "Where do I want others to be?" The principles and tools become the methods and means to get to dialogue.

HOW TO PREPARE FOR A CRUCIAL CONVERSATION

Here's one last tool to help you organize what we've shared about mastering crucial conversations. This tool will help you prepare for an upcoming crucial conversation or learn from one that you've already held.

Take a look at the table entitled Coaching for Crucial Conversations, which follows. The first column in the table lists the seven dialogue principles we've shared. The second column summarizes the skills associated with each principle. The final column is the best place to start coaching yourself or others. This column includes a list of questions that will help you apply specific skills to your conversations.

Coaching for Crucial Conversations

Principle	Skill	Crucial Question
1. Start with Heart (Chapter 3)	Focus on what you really want.	What am I acting like I really want? What do I really want? • For me? • For others? • For the relationship? How would I behave if I really did want this?
	Refuse the Sucker's Choice.	What do I *not* want? How should I go about getting what I really want and avoiding what I don't want?
2. Learn to Look (Chapter 4)	Look for when the conversation becomes crucial. Look for saftey problems. Look for our own Style Under Stress.	Am I going to silence or violence? Are others?

Coaching for Crucial Conversations (Continued)

Principle	Skill	Crucial Question
3. Make It Safe (Chapter 5)	Apologize when appropriate. Contrast to fix misunderstanding. CRIB to get to Mutual Purpose.	Why is safety at risk? • Have I established Mutual Purpose? • Am I maintaining Mutual Respect? What will I do to rebuild safety?
4. Master My Stories (Chapter 6)	Retrace my Path to Action. Separate fact from story. Watch for Three Clever Stories.	What is my story?
	Tell the rest of the story.	What am I pretending not to know about my role in the problem? Why would a reasonable, rational, and decent person do this? What should I do right now to move toward what I really want?
5. STATE My Path (Chapter 7)	Share your facts. Tell your story. Ask for others' paths. Talk tentatively. Encourage testing.	Am I really open to others' views? Am I talking about the real issue? Am I confidently expressing my own views?
6. Explore Others' Paths (Chapter 8)	Ask. Mirror. Paraphrase. Prime.	Am I actively exploring others' views?

Coaching for Crucial Conversations (Continued)

Principle	Skill	Crucial Question
	Agree. Build. Compare.	Am I avoiding unnecessary disagreement?
7. Move to Action (Chapter 9)	Decide how you'll decide. Document decisions and follow up.	How will we make decisions? Who will do what by when? How will we follow up?

Let's See How It All Works

We've included an extended case here to show how these principles might look when you find yourself in the middle of a crucial conversation. It outlines a tough discussion between you and your sister about dividing your mother's estate. The case is set up to illustrate where the principles apply, and to briefly review each principle as it comes up in the conversation.

The conversation begins with you bringing up the family summerhouse. Your mother's funeral was a month ago, and now it's time to split up both money and keepsakes. You're not really looking forward to it.

The issue is made touchier by the fact that you feel that since you almost single-handedly cared for your mother during the last several years, you should be compensated. You don't think your sister will see things the same way.

Your Crucial Conversation

> YOU: We have to sell the summer cottage. We never use it, and we need the cash to pay for my expenses from taking care of Mom the past four years.

SISTER: Please don't start with the guilt. I sent you money every month to help take care of Mom. If I didn't have to travel for my jobs, you know I would have wanted her at my house.

You notice that emotions are already getting strong. You're getting defensive, and your sister seems to be angry. You're in a crucial conversation, and it's not going well.

Start with Heart

Ask yourself what you really want. You want to be compensated fairly for the extra time and money you put in that your sister didn't. You also want to keep a good relationship with your sister. But you want to avoid making a Sucker's Choice. So you ask yourself: "How can I tell her that I want to be compensated fairly for the extra effort and expense I put in *and* keep a good relationship?"

Learn to Look

You recognize a lack of Mutual Purpose—you're both trying to defend your actions rather than discuss the estate.

Make It Safe

Contrast to help your sister understand your purpose.

YOU: I don't want to start an argument or try to make you feel guilty. But I do want to talk about being compensated for shouldering most of the responsibility over the last few years. I love Mom, but it put quite a strain on me financially and emotionally.

SISTER: What makes you think you did so much more than I did?

Master My Stories

You're telling yourself that you deserve more because you did more to care for your mother and covered unplanned expenses. Retrace your Path to Action to find out what facts are behind the story you're telling that's making you angry.

STATE My Path

You need to share your facts and conclusions with your sister in a way that will make her feel safe telling her story.

> YOU: It's just that I spent a lot of money taking care of Mom and did a lot of work caring for her instead of bringing in a nurse. I know you cared about Mom too, but I honestly feel like I did more in the day-to-day caregiving than you did, and it only seems fair to use some of what she left us to repay a part of what I spent. Do you see it differently? I'd really like to hear.

> SISTER: Okay, fine. Why don't you just send me a bill.

It sounds as though your sister isn't really okay with this arrangement. You can tell her voice is tense and her tone is one of giving in, not of true agreement.

Explore Others' Paths

Since part of your objective is to maintain a good relationship with your sister, it's important that she add her meaning to the pool. Use the AMPP skills to actively explore her views.

> YOU: The way you say that makes it sound like maybe that suggestion isn't okay with you. [*Mirror*] Is there something I'm missing? [*Ask*]

> SISTER: No—if you feel like you deserve more than I do, you're probably right.

YOU: Do you think I'm being unfair? That I'm not acknowledging your contributions? [*Prime*]

SISTER: It's just that I know I wasn't around much in the last couple of years. I've had to travel a lot for work. But I still visited whenever I could, and I sent money every month to help contribute to Mom's care. I offered to help pay to bring in a nurse if you thought it was necessary. I didn't know you felt you had an unfair share of the responsibility, and it seems like your asking for more money is coming out of nowhere.

YOU: So you feel like you were doing everything you could to help out and are surprised that I feel like I should be compensated? [*Paraphrase*]

SISTER: Well, yes.

Explore Others' Paths

You understand your sister's story now and still disagree to a point. Use the ABC skills to explain how your view differs. You agree in part with how your sister sees things. Use building to emphasize what you agree with and to bring up what you differ on.

YOU: You're right. You did a lot to help out, and I realize that it was expensive to visit as often as you did. I opted not to pay for professional home health care because Mom was more comfortable with me taking care of her, and I didn't mind that. On top of that, there were some incidental expenses it doesn't sound like you were aware of. The new medication she was on during the last eighteen months was twice as expensive as the old, and the insurance only covered a percentage of her hospital stays. It adds up.

SISTER: So it's these expenses you're worried about covering? Could we go over these expenses to decide how to cover them?

Move to Action

You want to create a definite plan for being reimbursed for these expenses, and you want it to be one you both agree on. Come to a consensus about what will happen, and document *who* does *what* by *when,* and settle on a way to *follow up.*

YOU: I've kept a record of all the expenses that went over the amount that both of us agreed to contribute. Can we sit down tomorrow to go over those and talk about what's fair to reimburse me for?

SISTER: Okay. We'll talk about the estate and write up a plan for how to divide things up.

SUMMARY—PUTTING IT ALL TOGETHER

If we first learn to recognize when safety is at risk and a conversation becomes crucial (Learn to Look) and that we need to take steps to Make It Safe for everyone to contribute his or her meaning, we can begin to see where to apply the skills we've learned. A visual model can also help us see where the principles and skills are needed.

Using these tools and reminders will get us started in mastering the skills that help us improve our crucial conversations.

11

Yeah, But

Advice for Tough Cases

As we (the authors) have taught this material, we've grown accustomed to people saying, "Yeah, but my situation's more difficult than that!" Or "Yeah, but the people I deal with aren't so quick to come around. Besides, most of the problems I face come as a surprise. I'm caught off guard." In short, people can think of a dozen reasons why the skills we've been talking about don't apply to the situations they care about.

- "Yeah, but what if someone does something that's really subtle? It drives you crazy but it's hard to identify. How do you handle that?"

- "Yeah, but what if my life partner refuses to ever talk about anything important? You can't force a person into dialogue."

- "Yeah, but what if I can't calm down quickly enough? I've been told not to go to bed angry, but sometimes I think I need time alone. What should I do?"

- "Yeah, but what if I don't trust the other person? How am I supposed to deal with that?"

- "Yeah, but both my boss and spouse are too sensitive to take any feedback. Shouldn't I just let things slide?"

In truth, the dialogue skills we've shared apply to just about any problem you can imagine. However, since some are more difficult than others, we've chosen seventeen tough cases. We'll take a moment to share a thought or two on each.

SEXUAL OR OTHER HARASSMENT

"YEAH, BUT... *IT'S NOT LIKE ANYONE'S BLATANTLY harassing me or anything, but I don't like the way I'm being treated. How can I bring it up without making enemies?"*

The Danger Point

Someone is making comments or gestures that you find offensive. The person does it seldom enough and he or she's subtle enough that you're not sure if HR or your boss can even help. What can you do?

In these situations it's easy to think that the offender has all the power. It seems as if the rules of polite society make it so that others can behave inappropriately and you end up looking like you're overreacting if you bring it up.

Generally speaking, a vast majority of these problems go away if they're privately, respectfully, and firmly discussed. Your biggest challenge will be the respect part. If you put up with this behavior for too long, you'll be inclined to tell a more and more potent Villain Story about the offender. This will jack up your emotions to the point that you'll go in with guns blazing—even if only through your body language.

The Solution

Tell the rest of the story. If you've tolerated the behavior for a long time before holding the conversation, own up to it. This may help you treat the individual like a reasonable, rational, and decent person—even if some of his or her behavior doesn't fit this description.

When you feel a measure of respect for the other person, you're ready to begin. After establishing a Mutual Purpose for the exchange, STATE your path. For example:

> "I'd like to talk about something that's getting in the way of my working with you. It's a tough issue to bring up, but I think it'll help us be better teammates if I do. Is that okay?" [*Establish Mutual Purpose*]
>
> "When I walk into your office, sometimes your eyes move up and down my body. And when I sit next to you at a computer, sometimes you put your arm around the back of my chair. I don't know that you're aware you're doing these things, so I thought I'd bring them up because they send a message that makes me uncomfortable. How do you see it?" [*STATE My Path*]

If you can be respectful and private but firm in this conversation, most problem behavior will stop. And remember, if the behavior is over the line, you shouldn't hesitate to contact HR to ensure your rights and dignity are protected.

MY OVERLY SENSITIVE SPOUSE

 "YEAH, BUT..." *WHAT DO YOU DO WHEN your spouse is too sensitive? You try to give him or her some constructive feedback, but he or she reacts so strongly that you end up going to silence."*

The Danger Point

Often couples come to an unspoken agreement during the first year or so of their marriage that affects how they communicate for the rest of their marriage. Say one person is touchy and can't take feedback, or the other doesn't give it very well. In any case, they in effect agree to say nothing to each other. They live in silence. Problems have to be huge before they're discussed.

The Solution

This is generally a problem of not knowing how to STATE your path. When something bothers you, catch it early. Contrasting can also help. "I'm not trying to blow this out of proportion. I just want to deal with it before it gets out of hand." Describe the specific behaviors you've observed. "When Jimmy leaves his room a mess, you use sarcasm to get his attention. You call him a 'pig' and then laugh as if you didn't mean it." Tentatively explain the consequences. "I don't think it's having the effect you want. He doesn't pick up on the hint, and I'm afraid that he's starting to resent you" (*Your story*). Encourage testing: "Do you see it differently?"

Finally, Learn to Look for signs that safety is at risk, and Make It Safe. When you STATE things well and others become defensive, refuse to conclude that the issue is impossible to discuss. Think harder about your approach. Step out of the content, do what it takes to make sure your partner feels safe, and then try again to candidly STATE your view.

When spouses stop giving each other helpful feedback, they lose out on the help of a lifelong confidant and coach. They miss out on hundreds of opportunities to help each other communicate more effectively.

FAILURE TO LIVE UP TO AGREEMENTS

 MY TEAMMATES ARE hypocrites. We get together and talk about all the ways we could improve, but then people don't do what they agreed to."

The Danger Point

The *worst* teams walk away from problems like these. In *good* teams, the boss eventually deals with problem behavior. In the *best* teams, every team member is part of the system of accountability. If team members see others violate a team agreement, they speak up immediately and directly. It's dangerous to wait for or expect the boss to do what good teammates should do themselves.

The Solution

If your teammate isn't doing what you think he or she should, it's up to you to speak up.

We realized this after watching a group of executives that agreed they'd hold off on all discretionary spending to help free up cash for a short-term crunch. This strategy sounded good in the warm glow of an off-site meeting, but the very next day a team member rushed back and prepaid a vendor for six months of consulting work—work that appeared to be "discretionary."

A team member who saw the executive prepare for and then make the prepayment didn't realize this was *the* crucial conversation that would determine whether the team would pull together or fall apart on this issue. Instead, he decided it was up to the boss to hold this person accountable. He said nothing. By the time the boss found out about the transaction and addressed the issue, the policy had already been violated and the money spent. Motivation to support the new plan dissipated, and the team ran short of cash.

When teams try to rally around aggressive change or bold new initiatives, they need to be prepared to address the problem when a team member doesn't live up to the agreement. Success does not depend on perfect compliance with new expectations, but on teammates who hold crucial conversations with one another when others appear to be reverting to old patterns.

DEFERENCE TO AUTHORITY

"YEAH, BUT...

PEOPLE WHO WORK FOR ME FILTER WHAT they say by guessing what they think I'm willing to hear. They take little initiative in solving important problems because they're afraid I'll disagree with them."

The Danger Point

When leaders face deference—or what feels like kissing up— they typically make one of two mistakes. Either they misdiagnose the cause (fear), or they try to banish deference with a brash command.

Misdiagnose. Often, leaders are causing the fear but denying it. "Who me? I don't do a thing to make people feel uncomfortable." They haven't Learned to Look. They're unaware of their Style Under Stress. Despite this disclaimer, the way they carry themselves, their habit of speaking in absolutes, their subtle use of authority—something out there—is creating fear and eventual deference.

Then there's the other misdiagnosis: leaders who face "head-bobbing kiss-ups" often think they're doing something wrong when, in fact, they're living with ghosts of previous leaders. They do their best to be open and supportive and to involve people, but despite their genuine efforts, people still keep their distance. Often, people treat their leaders like celebrities or dictators, regardless of the fact that they've done nothing to deserve it.

Before you do anything, you need to find out if you're the cause, if you're living with ghosts of bosses past, or both.

Command it away. Many leaders seek the simple path. They *tell* people to stop deferring.

> "It seems to me that you're agreeing with me because I'm the boss and not because what I'm saying makes sense."
> "Absolutely!"
> "I'd prefer that you stop deferring to me and simply listen to the idea."
> "Okay. whatever you say, Boss!"

With ingrained deference you face a catch-22. If you don't say something, it'll probably continue. If you do say something, you may be inadvertently encouraging it to continue.

The Solution

Work on me first. Discover your part in the problem. Don't ask your direct reports. If they're already deferring to you, they'll whitewash the problem. Consult with a peer who watches you in action. Ask for honest feedback. Are you doing things that cause people to defer to you? If so, what? Explore your peer's path by having him or her point out your specific behaviors. Jointly develop a plan of attack, work on it, and seek continued feedback.

If the problem stems from ghosts (the actions of previous leaders), *go public*. Describe the problem in a group or team meeting and then ask for advice. Don't try to command it away. You can't. Reward risk takers. Encourage testing. When people do express an opinion contrary to yours, thank them for their honesty. Play devil's advocate. If you can't get others to disagree, then disagree with yourself. Let people know that all ideas are open to question. If you need to, leave the room. Give people some breathing space.

FAILED TRUST

"YEAH, BUT..."	*I DON'T KNOW WHAT to do. I'm not sure I can trust this person. He missed an important deadline. Now I wonder if I should trust him again."*

The Danger Point

People often assume that trust is something you have or don't have. Either you trust someone or you don't. That puts too much pressure on trust. "What do you mean I can't stay out past midnight? Don't you trust me?" your teenage son inquires.

Trust doesn't have to be universally offered. In truth, it's usually offered in degrees and is very topic specific. It also comes in two flavors—motive and ability. For example, you can trust me to administer CPR if needed; I'm motivated. But you can't trust me to do a good job; I know nothing about it.

The Solution

Deal with trust around the issue, not around the person.

When it comes to regaining trust in others, don't set the bar too high. Just try to trust them in the moment, not across all issues. You don't have to trust them in everything. To make it safe for yourself in the moment, bring up your concerns. Tentatively STATE what you see happening. "I get the sense that you're only sharing the good side of your plan. I need to hear the possible risks before I'm comfortable. Is that okay?" If they play games, call them on it.

Also, don't use your mistrust as a club to punish people. If they've earned your mistrust in one area, don't let it bleed over into your overall perception of their character. If you tell yourself a Villain Story that exaggerates others' untrustworthiness, you'll act in ways that help them justify themselves in being even less worthy of your trust. You'll start up a self-defeating cycle and get more of what you *don't* want.

WON'T TALK ABOUT ANYTHING SERIOUS

 MY SPOUSE IS THE person you talked about earlier. You know, I try to hold a meaningful discussion, I try to work through an important problem, and he or she simply withdraws. What can I do?"

The Danger Point

It's common to blame others for not wanting to stay in dialogue as if it were some kind of genetic disorder. That's not the problem. If others don't want to talk about tough issues, it's because they believe that it won't do any good. Either they aren't good at dialogue, or you aren't, or you both aren't—or so they think.

The Solution

Work on me first. Your spouse may have an aversion to all crucial conversations, even when talking to a skilled person. Nevertheless, you're still the only person you can work on. Start with simple challenges. Don't go for the really tough issues. Do your best to Make It Safe. Constantly watch to see when your spouse starts to become uncomfortable. Use tentative language. Separate intent from outcome. "I'm pretty sure you're not intending to . . ." If your spouse consistently seems unwilling to talk about his or her personal issues, learn how to Explore Others' Paths. Practice these skills every chance you get. In short, start simply and then bring all your dialogue tools into play.

Now, having said all of this, exercise patience. Don't nag. Don't lose hope and then go to violence. Every time you become aggressive or insulting, you give your spouse additional evidence that crucial conversations do nothing but cause harm.

If you're constantly on your best dialogue behavior, you'll build more safety in the relationship and your spouse will be more likely to begin picking up on the cues and start coming around.

When you see signs of improvement, you can accelerate the growth by inviting your spouse to talk with you about *how* you talk. Your challenge here is to build safety by establishing a compelling Mutual Purpose. You need to help your partner see a *reason* for having this conversation—a reason that is so compelling that he or she will be willing to take part.

Share what you think the consequences of having or not having this conversation could be (both positive and negative). Explain what it means to both you and the relationship. Then invite your spouse to help identify the topics you have a hard time discussing. Take turns describing how you both tend to approach these topics. Then discuss the possible benefits of helping each other make improvements.

Sometimes if you can't talk about the tough topics, you can more easily talk about *how* you talk—or don't talk—about them. That helps get things started.

VAGUE BUT ANNOYING

THE PERSON I'M THINKING OF doesn't do blatantly unacceptable things—nothing to write home about— just subtle stuff that's starting to drive me crazy."

The Danger Point

If people simply bother you at some abstract level, maybe what they're doing isn't worthy of a conversation. Perhaps the problem is not their behavior but your tolerance. For example, an executive laments, "My employees really disappoint me. Just look at the length of their hair." It turns out that the employees in question have no contact with anyone besides one another. Their hair length has nothing to do with job performance. The boss really has no reason to say anything.

However, when actions are both subtle *and* unacceptable, then you have to retrace your Path to Action and put your finger on exactly what others are doing or you have nothing to discuss. Abstract descriptions peppered with your vague conclusions or stories have no place in crucial conversations. For example, whenever your family gets together, your brother constantly takes potshots at everyone else using sarcastic humor. The individual comments aren't directly insulting enough to discuss. What you want to talk about is the fact that these constant comments make every get-together feel negative. Remember, clarifying the facts is the homework required for crucial conversations.

The Solution

Retrace your Path to Action to its source. Identify specific behaviors that are out of bounds and take note. When you've done your homework, consider the behaviors you noted and make sure the story you're telling yourself about these behaviors is important enough for dialogue. If it is, then Make It Safe and STATE Your Path.

SHOWS NO INITIATIVE

 SOME MEMBERS OF MY WORK TEAM do what they're asked, but no more. If they run into a problem, they take one simple stab at fixing it. But if their efforts don't pay off, they quit."

The Danger Point

Most people are far more likely to talk about the presence of a bad behavior than the absence of a good one. When someone really messes up, leaders and parents alike are compelled to take action. However, when people simply fail to be excellent, it's hard to know what to say.

The Solution

Establish new and higher expectations. Don't deal with a specific instance; deal with the overall pattern. If you want someone to show more initiative, tell him or her. Give specific examples of when the person ran into a barrier and then backed off after a single try. Raise the bar and then make it crystal clear what you've done. Jointly brainstorm what the person could have done to be both more persistent and more creative in coming up with a solution.

For instance, "I asked you to finish up a task that absolutely had to be completed before I returned from a trip. You ran into a problem, tried to get in touch with me, and then simply left a message with my four-year-old. What could you have done to track me down on the road?" or "What would it have taken to create a backup strategy?"

Pay attention to ways you are compensating for someone's lack of initiative. Have you made yourself responsible for following up? If so, talk with that person about assuming this responsibility. Have you asked more than one person to take the same assignment so you can be sure it will get done? If so, talk to the person originally assigned about reporting progress to you early so you only need to put someone else on the job when there's a clear need for more resources.

Stop *acting out* your expectations that others won't take initiative. Instead, talk your expectations out and come to agreements that place the responsibility on the team members while giving you information early enough that you aren't left high and dry.

SHOWS A PATTERN

"YEAH, BUT... *IT ISN'T A SINGLE PROBLEM. It's that I keep having to talk with people about the same problem. I feel like I have to choose between being a nag and putting up with the problem. Now what?"*

The Danger Point

Some crucial conversations go poorly because you're having the wrong conversations. You talk to someone who is late for a meeting for the second time. Then the third. Your blood begins to boil. Then you bite your lip and give another gentle reminder. Finally, after your resentment builds up (because you're telling yourself an ugly story), you become violent. You make a sarcastic or cutting comment and then end up looking stupid because the reaction seems way out of line given the minor offense.

If you continue to return to the original problem (coming in late) without talking about the new problem (failing to live up to commitments), you're stuck in "Groundhog Day." We talk about this problem using the *Groundhog Day* movie metaphor. If you return to the same initial problem, you're like Bill Murray in the movie—you're forced to relive the same situation over and over rather than deal with the bigger problem. Nothing ever gets resolved.

The Solution

Learn to Look for patterns. Don't focus exclusively on a single event. Watch for behavior over time. Then STATE Your Path by talking about the pattern. For example, if a person is late for meetings and agrees to do better, the next conversation should not be about tardiness. It should be about his or her failure to keep a commitment. This is a bigger issue. It's now about trust and respect.

People often become far more emotional than the issue they're discussing warrants because they're talking about the wrong issue. If you're really bothered because of a pattern, but you're talking about this latest instance, your emotions will seem out of proportion. In contrast, an interesting thing happens when you hold the *right* conversation. Your emotions calm down. When you talk about what's really eating you—the pattern—you'll be able to be more composed and effective.

Don't get pulled into any one instance or your concern will seem trivial. Talk about the overall pattern.

I NEED TIME TO CALM DOWN!

 I'VE BEEN TOLD THAT I should never go to bed angry. Is that always a good idea?"

The Danger Point

Once you've become angry, it's not always easy to calm down. You've told yourself an ugly story, your body has responded by preparing for a fight, and now you're trying your best not to duke it out—only your body hasn't caught up with your brain. So what do you do? Do you try to stay in dialogue even though your intuition tells you to back off and buy some time? After all, Mom said, "Never go to bed angry."

The Solution

Okay, so your mom wasn't exactly right. She was right by suggesting that you shouldn't let serious problems go unresolved.

She was wrong about always sticking with a discussion, no matter your emotional state. It's perfectly okay to suggest that you need some time alone and that you'd like to pick up the discussion later on—say, tomorrow. Then, after you've dissipated the adrenaline and have had time to think about the issues, hold the conversation. Coming to mutual agreement to take a time-out is not the same thing as going to silence. In fact, it's a very healthy example of dialogue.

As a sidenote on this topic, it's not such a good idea to tell others that they need to calm down or that they need to take some time out. They may need the time, but it's hard to suggest it without coming off as patronizing. "Take ten minutes, calm down, and then get back to me." With others, get back to the source of their anger. Retrace their Path to Action.

ENDLESS EXCUSES

 MY TEENAGE SON is a master of excuses. I talk to him about a problem, and he's always got a new reason why it's not his fault."

The Danger Point

It's easy to be lulled into a series of never-ending excuses—particularly if the other person doesn't want to do what you've asked and learns that as long as he or she can give you a plausible reason, all bets are off.

I go to work before my son leaves for school, and he's constantly late. First he told me that he was late because his alarm broke. The next day the old car we bought him had a problem—or so he says. Then his friend forgot to pick him up. Then he had a head cold and couldn't hear his new alarm. Then . . ."

The Solution

With "imaginative" people, take a preemptive strike against all new excuses. Gain a commitment to solve the overall problem, not simply the stated cause. For instance, the first time the person is late, seek a commitment to fix the alarm—*and anything else that might stand in the way.* Repairing the alarm only deals with one potential cause. Ask the person to deal with the problem—being late.

> "So you think that if you get a new alarm, you'll be able to make it to school on time? That's fine with me. Do whatever it takes to get there on time. Can I count on you being there tomorrow at eight o'clock sharp?"

Then remember, as the excuses accumulate, don't talk about the most recent excuse; talk about the pattern.

INSUBORDINATION (OR OVER-THE-LINE DISRESPECT)

 WHAT IF THE PEOPLE you talk to not only are angry, but also become insubordinate? How do you handle that?"

The Danger Point

When you're discussing a tough issue with employees (or even your kids), there's always the chance they'll step over the line. They'll move from a friendly dispute to a heated discussion and then into the nasty territory of being insubordinate or acting disrespectful.

The trouble is, insubordination is so rare that it takes most leaders by surprise. So they buy time to figure out what to do. And in so doing, they let the person get away with something that was way out of line. Worse still, their perceived indifference makes them an accomplice to all future abuses. Parents, on the other hand, caught by surprise, tend to respond in kind, becoming angry and insulting.

The Solution

Show zero tolerance for insubordination. Speak up immediately, but respectfully. Change topics from the issue at hand to how the person is currently acting. Catch the escalating disrespect before it turns into abuse and insubordination. Let the person know that his or her passion for the issue at hand is leading down a dangerous trail. "I'd like to step away from this scheduling issue for a moment—then we'll come right back to it. The way you're leaning in toward me and raising your voice seems disrespectful. I want to help address your concerns, but I'm going to have a tough time doing so if this continues."

If you can't catch it early, discuss the insubordination and seek help from HR specialists.

REGRETTING SAYING SOMETHING HORRIBLE

"YEAH, BUT... *SOMETIMES I LET A PROBLEM go for a long time, and then when I bring it up, I say something just awful. How do I recover from this?"*

The Danger Point

When other people do things that bother us, and then we tell ourselves a story about how they're bad and wrong, we're setting ourselves up for an unhealthy conversation. Of course, when we tell ourselves an ugly story and then sit on it, it only gets worse. Stories left unattended don't get better with time—they ferment. Then, when we eventually can't take it anymore, we say something we regret.

The Solution

First, don't repress your story. Use your STATE skills early on, before the story turns too ugly. Second, if you have let the problem build, don't hold the crucial conversation while angry. Set aside a time when you can discuss it in a calm fashion. Then, using your STATE skills, explain what you've seen and heard, and tentatively tell the most simple and least offensive story. "The way you just told me that our neighbor thinks I'm a real idiot has me worried. You smiled and laughed when you said it. I'm beginning to wonder if you take pleasure in running to me with negative feedback. Is that what's going on?"

If you do say something horrible—"You're cruel, you know that? You love to hurt me and I'm sick of it"—apologize. You can't unring the bell, but you can apologize. Then STATE Your Path.

TOUCHY AND PERSONAL

"YEAH, BUT... *WHAT IF SOMEONE has a hygiene problem? Or maybe someone's boring and people avoid him or her. How could you ever talk about something personal and sensitive like that?"*

The Danger Point

Most people avoid sensitive issues like the plague. Who can blame them? Unfortunately, when fear and misapplied compassion rule over honesty and courage, people can go for years without being given information that could be extremely helpful.

When people do speak up, they often leap from silence to violence. Jokes, nicknames, and other veiled attempts to sneak in vague feedback are both indirect and disrespectful. Also, the longer you go without saying anything, the greater the pain when you finally deliver the message.

The Solution

Use Contrasting. Explain that you don't want to hurt the person's feelings, but you do want to share something that could be helpful. Establish Mutual Purpose. Let the other person know your intentions are honorable. Also explain that you're reluctant to bring up the issue because of its personal nature, but since the problem is interfering with the person's effectiveness, you really must. Tentatively describe the problem. Don't play it up or pile it on. Describe the specific behaviors and then move to solutions. Although these discussions are never easy, they certainly don't have to be offensive or insulting.

WORD GAMES

 MY CHILDREN are constantly playing word games. If I try to tell them that they shouldn't have done something, they say I never told them exactly that. They're starting to get on my nerves."

The Danger Point

Sometimes parents (and leaders) are tricked into accepting poor performance by silver-tongued individuals who are infinitely creative in coming up with new ways to explain why they didn't know any better. Not only do these inventive people have the ability to conjure up creative excuses, but they also have the energy and will to do so incessantly. Eventually they wear you down. As a result, they get away with doing less or doing it poorly, while hard-working, energetic family members (or employees) end up carrying an unfair share of the load.

The Solution

This is another case of pattern over instance. Tentatively STATE the pattern of splitting hairs and playing word games. Let them know they aren't fooling anyone. In this case, don't focus exclusively on actions, because creative people can always find new inappropriate actions. "You didn't say I couldn't call her 'stupid.'" Talk about both behaviors and outcomes. "You're hurting your sister's feelings when you call her stupid. Please don't do that, or anything else that might hurt her feelings."

Use previous behavior as an example, and then hold them accountable to results. Don't get pulled into discussing any one instance. Stick with the pattern.

NO WARNING

"YEAH, BUT..." I'VE GOT A LOT OF GOOD people working for me, but they're too full of surprises. When they run into problems, I only find out after it's too late. They always have a good excuse, so what should I do?"

The Danger Point

Leaders who are constantly being surprised allow it to happen. The first time an employee says, "Sorry, but I ran into a problem," the leaders miss the point. They listen to the problem, work on it, and then move on to a new topic. In so doing, they are saying: "It's okay to surprise me. If you have a legitimate excuse, stop what you're doing, turn your efforts to something else, and then wait until I show up to spring the news."

The Solution

Make it perfectly clear that once you've given an assignment, there are only two acceptable paths. Employees need to complete the assignment as planned, or if they run into a problem, they need to immediately inform you. No surprises. Similarly, if they decide that another job needs to be done instead, they call you. No surprises.

Clarify the "no surprises" rule. The first time someone comes back with a legitimate excuse—but he or she didn't tell you when the problem first came up—deal with this as the new problem. "We agreed that you'd let me know immediately. I didn't get a call. What happened?"

DEALING WITH SOMEONE WHO BREAKS ALL THE RULES

 "YEAH, BUT..." *WHAT IF THE PERSON you're dealing with violates all of the dialogue principles most of the time—especially during crucial conversations."*

The Danger Point

When you look at a continuum of dialogue skills, most of us (by definition) fall in the middle. Sometimes we're on and sometimes we're off. Some of us are good at avoiding Sucker's Choices; others are good at making it safe. Of course, you have the extremes as well. You have people who are veritable conversational geniuses. And now you're saying that you work with (maybe live with) someone who is the complete opposite. He or she rarely uses any skills. What's a person to do?

The danger, of course, is that the other person isn't as bad as you think—you bring out the worst in him or her—or that he or she really is that bad, and you try to address all the problems at once.

The Solution

Let's assume this person is pretty bad all of the time and with most everyone. Where do you start? Let's apply a metaphor here. How do you eat an elephant? One bite at a time. Choose your targets very carefully. Consider two dimensions: (1) What bothers you the most? "He or she is constantly assuming the worst and telling horrible stories." (2) What might be the easiest to work on? "He or she rarely shows any appreciation."

Look for those areas that are most grievous to you and might not be all that hard to talk about. Pick one element and work on it. Establish Mutual Purpose. Frame the conversation in a way that the other person will care about.

> "I love it when we're feeling friendly toward each other. I'd like to have that feeling more frequently between us. There are a couple of things I'd like to talk about that I'm pretty convinced would help us with that. Can we talk?"

STATE the issue, and then work on that one issue. Don't nag; don't take on everything at once. Deal with one element, one day at a time.

12

Change Your Life
How to Turn Ideas into Habits

One day you "overhear" yourself enthusiastically talking about a professional wrestling match. You're speaking with such gusto that you give yourself the willies. You think to yourself: "You know what? It's time to expand my cultural horizons." So you vow to read more widely and to watch three programs on the science channel for every episode of reality TV.

While you're at it, you commit to trimming down a bit as well. A reasonable diet and moderate exercise program couldn't hurt. To top it all off, you note that you're nearly consumed with your work, so you swear to spend more time with your family.

More culture, better health, a stronger family—certainly you'll quickly transform such worthy desires into daily habits.

Hardly. Changes of this sort are rarely easy. When it comes to turning our wispy hopes into concrete realities, our success rate is mixed at best. This being the case, what are our chances of improving something as deeply rooted in our psyches as the way we communicate? Actually, it depends. There are a lot of variables that affect our chances. Consider the following factors.

SURPRISE

You've been asked to conduct your first meeting. To avoid embarrassing yourself, you read a book where you learn all about agendas, pacing, and the like. When it's time to lead your first meeting, you arrive early, adjust the chairs, set the markers just so, and lay out an agenda for each participant. As participants arrive, you greet them cordially. Then you kick off the meeting with a rousing icebreaker and you're off and running.

Implementing meeting skills is as easy as falling off a log. That's because meetings are evident. You know when you're in one. You're seated at a table along with a bunch of other people. How could you not know you're in a meeting? They're also predictable. You can plan for them. You even have time to go over underlined portions from the book.

Crucial conversations, in contrast, are far less evident. You don't sit in a crucial conversations room. You don't pass around a picture of your Path to Action. Instead you get thrown into a heated discussion where you rarely think, "Oh yes, I'm in the middle of a crucial conversation. That means I need to think about all that stuff I read last week."

Discussions are also less predictable. Nobody sends you an invitation stating: "Would you please engage me in a crucial conversation next week after the team meeting where you're going to make a policy that will miff me?" High-risk discussions don't come with notices and reminders. More often than not, they come as unwelcome surprises.

EMOTION

Emotions don't help much either. And, of course, crucial conversations are defined by their emotional characteristics. Your ability to pull yourself out of the content of a discussion and to focus on the process is inversely proportional to your level of emotion. The more you care about what's happening, the less likely you are to think about how you're conducting yourself.

It's almost unfair. The bigger the deal, the less likely you are to bring your newly acquired skill-set into the conversation. Like it or not, if your adrenaline is flowing, you're almost guaranteed to jump to your Style Under Stress.

Between surprise and emotion, it's hard to know which is the bigger enemy of change. Both make it hard to remember to act in new ways.

SCRIPTS

Now let's look at still another enemy of change—scripts. Scripts are prebundled phrases we use in common conversations; they form the very foundation of social habits and often make change almost impossible. Consider the following.

When we learn to speak, first come words, then phrases, and then scripts. The larger the bundles of words we carry around, the less we have to worry about combining them into sensible expressions. Also the less we have to fret over syntax or grammar—that work has already been done for us.

Unfortunately, predetermined expressions also put us into a sort of mental autopilot. Consider what happens when you walk into a fast-food restaurant. Do you think about the words you'll choose? Probably not. That's because when you enter familiar circumstances, you're carrying not only words and phrases, but an entire *script* in your head.

With a script, you know *both sides* of the conversation. You know that the person at the counter is going to ask for your order. You're certain that the perky young woman with the paper hat is going to ask you if you want fries. Even if you include fries in your original request, she's still going to ask, "Do you want fries with that?" And if you say yes, you can bet the farm that she's going to ask, "Do you want to super-size that?"

The good news about packing around scripts is that you don't have to give conversation much thought. The bad news is that the more scripted an interaction, the more difficult it is to pull yourself out of the routine and try something new. For example, as you walk up to a fast-food counter, your spouse reminds you to ask for extra ketchup.

You step up to the counter and say: "I'll have two house specials, three kiddy delights . . ." and then you slip into autopilot. The words that pour out of your mouth have no relation to your thoughts. Your brain is somewhere else entirely. You're musing over a menu that sports a sandwich made out of "ribs" that have no bones. "What poor animal has boneless ribs?" you're thinking to yourself.

And guess what? As you robotically state your order, one word spilling out after another, you forget to ask for extra ketchup. What do you expect from a person who's devoting no real brain time to the interaction? In fact, your spouse's request never even makes it onto your radar screen—which is currently filled with images of Jell-O-like, ribless creatures mooing and slithering across a backdrop painted by Salvador Dali.

Scripts place us on a smooth and familiar track. They take us across known territory and at a comfortable pace—freeing our brains for more novel work. But then again, when we're on rails, we travel along the prescribed route with such finesse and ease that it's almost impossible to make an unscheduled turn.

WHAT ARE OUR CHANCES?

So let's see what we're facing when we try to change our Style Under Stress. Tough conversations come at us out of nowhere, fill us with adrenaline, and evoke comfortable (but not necessarily good) routines. They are spontaneous, emotional, and backed by years of practice.

Consequently, when you examine people working through crucial conversations, they look a lot more like racehorses charging out of the gate than human beings making choices. Conversationalists are shocked into motion by surprise, whipped up to speed by high stakes and strong emotions, and propelled along a completely predictable course by scripts that offer few if any options.

TRANSFER TIPS

Given the challenges of altering routine scripts, can people actually change? Early in our research, we (the authors) once examined forty-eight front-line supervisors who were learning how to hold crucial conversations. As we watched the trainees back at work, it became clear to us that only a few of them transferred what they had learned in the classroom back to their work site. The bad news is that most of them didn't change an iota. The good news is that some of them did. In fact, they used the new skills precisely as instructed.

The supervisors who found a way to apply the new skills taught us the following four principles for turning ideas into action:

- *First, master the content.* That means not only do you have to be able to recognize what works and why, but you have to generate new scripts of your own.

- *Second, master the skills.* You must be able to enact these new scripts in a way that is consistent with the supporting principles. As it turns out, simply understanding a concept isn't enough. While it's helpful, even necessary to talk the talk, you have to be able to *walk* the talk. You have to be able to say the right words with the right tone and nonverbal actions. When it comes to social skills, knowing and doing are two different animals.

- *Third, enhance your motive.* You must want to change. This means that you have to care enough about improving your crucial conversation skills to actually do something. You have to move from a passive sense that it would be a good idea to change, to an active desire to seek opportunities. Ability without motive lies dormant and untapped.

- *Fourth, watch for cues.* To overcome surprise, emotion, and scripts, you must recognize the call to action. This is usually people's biggest obstacle to change. Old stimuli generate old responses. If a problem doesn't cue your new skills, you'll return to your old habits without even realizing you missed a chance to try something new.

Master the Content

There's too much material in this book to try to master in one sitting. Despite the fact that you may have read this book rather quickly, a rapid once-over rarely generates much of a change in behavior. You may have a feel for the content, but probably not enough to propel you to change.

Here are some other steps you can take to help master the content.

Do something. Years ago, Dale Carnegie recommended that you read his now classic *How to Win Friends and Influence People* one chapter at a time. Then, once you finished the chapter, he suggested you go out and practice what you learned from it. We agree. Pick a chapter you found relevant (possibly one with a low score in your Style Under Stress test) and read it again. This time, implement what you learned over a three- to five-day period. Look for opportunities. Pounce on every chance you get. Step up to the plate and give the skills a try. Then pick another chapter and repeat the process.

Discuss the material. When you first learn something, your knowledge is "preverbal." That is, you might recognize the concepts if you see them, but you're not able to discuss them with ease. You haven't talked about them enough to make them part of your functional vocabulary. You haven't turned the words into phrases and the phrases into scripts. To move your knowledge to the next level, read a chapter and then discuss it with a friend or loved one. Talk about the material until the concepts come naturally.

Teach the material. If you really want to master a concept, teach it to someone else. Stick with it until the other person understands the concept well enough to pass it on to someone else.

Master the Skills

There's a story going around the self-help talk circuit about a Vietnam War prisoner who played golf in his head in order to help maintain his sanity. He'd mentally step up to each hole at his favorite golf course and "play" an entire round. After being released, he eventually found his way to the course, where he promptly shot his best score ever, one under par. When his friends acted astonished at his new-found talent, he explained,

"Why shouldn't I have shot under par? I never once shot over par while I was in prison."

This tale is routinely used to teach the power of mental preparation. Gurus can't say enough about the power of the mental game. While we agree that *thinking* is an essential part of the process, we'd like to emphasize the greater importance of *doing*. Evidence suggests that mental preparation can make some difference in execution, but thinking isn't enough. If you really want to improve your ability, practice. Step up to problems and give the material a try.

Rehearse with a friend. Start by rehearsing with a friend. Ask a colleague or coworker to partner with you. Explain that you'd like to practice the skills you're learning. Briefly discuss the skill you'll be attempting. Provide the details of a real problem you're facing. (Don't include names or otherwise violate privacy issues.) Next, ask your friend to play the role of the other person and practice the crucial conversation.

Ask your partner to give you honest feedback. Otherwise you could be practicing the wrong delivery. Remember, practice doesn't make perfect; *perfect* practice makes perfect. Insist that your practice partner hold you to a high standard. Make sure you're constantly improving.

Practice on the fly. You're going to be holding crucial conversations at home and at work, or you wouldn't have bought this book in the first place. So practice the skills you've been reading, teaching, and rehearsing. If you have children, hardly a day will pass that you won't have a chance to practice.

Start immediately. If you wait until you're perfect before you give something a try, you could be waiting a long time. To make it safe, pick a conversation of only medium risk. Trying out something new is hard enough without applying it to a monumental problem.

Practice in a training session. For those of you who would like more material and practice opportunities than you can extract from a book and other static materials, attend one of our live training seminars. Give us a call and see if you can either schedule a session at a location near you or bring the training into your company.

Our training materials library is equipped with a variety of delivery tools ranging from leader-guided workshops to off-site intensive courses.

Enhance Your Motive

We all have ideas about how to motivate others, but how do you motivate yourself? While you may feel 100 percent committed to improving your crucial conversations right now, what can you do when you're staring at an angry coworker and your commitment to improvment drops to, say, 10 percent?

The truth is that we often need to take steps to ensure that our most well-founded wishes (those made during peaceful moments where we're taking an honest look at the future) survive turbulent, less forward-looking circumstances.

Apply incentives. Start with the obvious. Use incentives. For example, people going through self-help courses are often encouraged to put their money where their mouth is. Every time they fulfill an assignment, they're given back a portion of their tuition. On the other hand, if they don't step up, it costs them. When incentives are added, results improve fairly dramatically.

So every time you deftly hold a crucial conversation, celebrate your victory. Treat yourself to something you wouldn't otherwise enjoy. And don't wait for perfection. Celebrate improvement. If you used to get in a heated argument every time you brought up a certain problem, and now the interaction is merely tense, enjoy the victory. Self-improvement is achieved by individuals who appreciate direction more than those who demand perfection.

Apply disincentives. You might consider disincentives as well. Take a look at what went on at Stanford a few years back. Subjects who were trying to lose weight were asked to write a donation check to an organization they despised. These checks were then set aside, never to be mailed unless the subjects failed to live up to their goals—at which point five hundred dollars was sent to Americans for Nuclear Proliferation or something equally distasteful to the subject. As predicted, subjects did better when they used disincentives.[1]

Go public. Let others know that you're trying to routinely hold crucial conversations. Explain what you're doing and why. Over half a century ago, Dr. Kurt Lewin, the father of social psychology, learned that when subjects made a public commitment to do something, they were more likely to stay the course than if they kept their wishes to themselves.[2] Tell people what your goals are. Get social pressure working in your favor.

Talk with your boss. If you want to take it a step further, sit down with your boss and explain your goals. Ask for his or her support. If you want to put some real teeth into your goal, build your plan into your performance review. As a leader, you're almost always asked to pick one "soft area" listed on your performance review forms and work on it. Select dialogue. You might as well tie your plans for improvement into the formal reward system. Align your personal, family, and organizational goals to a single goal—improving your dialogue skills.

Remember the costs; focus on the reward. Perhaps the most predictive piece of social science research ever conducted was completed with small children and marshmallows. A child was put in a room and then told that he or she could have either one marshmallow now or two if he or she was willing to wait until the adult returned in a few minutes. The adult would then place one marshmallow in front of the child and exit. Some of the children delayed gratification. Others ate the marshmallow right away. Researchers continued studying these children.

Over the next several decades, the children who had delayed gratification ended up doing far better in life than those who hadn't. They had stronger marriages, made more money, and were healthier.[3] This willingness to do without now in order to achieve more later turns out to be an all-purpose tool for success.

How did the children who were able to delay gratification fight off their short-term wishes? First, they looked away from the scrumptious marshmallow that sat in front of them. No use torturing themselves with the vision of what they couldn't have. Second, they kept telling themselves that if they waited, they would get two, not one. What could be simpler?

As you step up to a crucial conversation and wonder if it's really worth trying out something new and untested, remind yourself why you're trying new skills in the first place. Focus on improved results. Remember what happens when you fall back on your old methods.

Think "things." How can *things* help motivate you? Actually, this particular concept isn't easy to grasp. An example might help. You're unsuccessfully trying to lose weight. It turns out that your early-morning iron will turns into midday rubber as your stomach begins to growl and you sniff the air of the restaurant you frequent for lunch. What can you do with *things* to help keep you on track?

Pack a sensible lunch first thing in the morning when your will is strong. Take no money with you. That way it won't be easy to cave in to your weaker, afternoon wishes. By structuring around your self-control cycles, you heighten the power of your stronger motives while lessening the blow of you weaker moments.

Schedule crucial conversations when you're feeling confident. Practice beforehand. Take notes. Set up your office the way you would like. Armed with smart timing and material support, you're far more likely to step up to tough problems effectively.

Build in Cues

To remind yourself to use your new skills, create helpful cues.

Mark hot spots. People who go through stress-reduction training learn to mark physical items that are closely linked to their sources of tension. People who freak out in traffic put a small red circle on their steering wheel. Individuals who are constantly in a rush put one on their watch.

When it comes to the tough conversations you face, you might want to make use of small visual cues as well. Place one on the computer that spits out results that drive you nuts. Build a cue into your copy of the agenda of any meeting that typically serves up tough problems.

Set aside a time. Perhaps the best way to remind yourself to use your new skills is to set aside a time each day to walk around in search of both successes and problems. When you see a success, celebrate. When you encounter a problem, bring your best dialogue tools into play.

Read reactions. If you're not doing a good job of holding crucial conversations, the results are going to be right in front of you. If you see that you're getting off track, back up and start over. Use real-life cues (e.g., the other person's jaw tenses, he or she clams up, etc.) to remind yourself that maybe it's time to try a new tactic. If necessary, apologize. Move to an earlier place in the discussion and follow the process.

Build in permanent reminders. Order a poster of the model, place it on the wall, and look at it each morning as you start the day.

Carry a reminder. Along with the poster, order a set of cue cards you can tuck into your purse or shirt pocket.

A DIGITAL ASSIST

We've tried to include in this book everything you'll need to conduct crucial conversations. Our goal was to provide a complete, stand-alone tool for personal change. Nevertheless, when it comes to improving social interactions, the digital domain has a lot to offer as well. Audio, video, and other digital tools can enhance your learning experience.

As an additional resource, we invite you to our website. There you'll find a variety of tools for helping you transform the printed word into daily actions. Digital tools include conceptual, behavioral, and cuing tools.

Conceptual Tools

Watch. To give you live-action views of the skills we cover, we've added video examples to our website. Visit us at www.crucial-conversations.com and check out video clips for specific skills.

Listen. Many people enjoy listening to audiotapes or CDs as they commute to and from work each day. We've put together an audio mastery course that not only reviews the material chapter by chapter, but also provides audio examples of what the skills sound like when put into action. Move your knowledge from the abstract to the concrete as you hear how the theories translate into words and the words build into usable scripts.

Behavioral Tools

If you'd like to practice specific skills with the aid of a role-play tool, go to our website and check out Free Resources to download role-play rehearsals. Print out the role plays and then work with a partner until you've mastered the skill.

Cuing Tools

Visit www.crucialconversations.com to sign up for regular tips, reminders, and other resources to keep you watching for opportunities to use your crucial conversations skills.

A PARTING THOUGHT

We'll be forever indebted to the wonderful people who allowed us to roll up our sleeves, work side by side with them, and study their best practices. We're particularly grateful to individuals who allowed us to watch them as they struggled to work through crucial conversations. It's hard enough to sort out facts, stories, and feelings without being scrutinized under a microscope while you're doing it.

We hope that by sharing the theories, skills, and models we've learned from these dear friends and colleagues, we'll help you feel more comfortable stepping up to your own crucial conversations. You'll be able to add to the pool of available meaning, make better decisions, and work in a way that both gets the job done *and* enhances your relationships.

So we encourage you to pick a relationship. Pick a conversation. Let others know that you're trying to do better, then give it a shot. When you blow it, admit it. Don't expect perfection; aim for progress. And when you succeed, celebrate your success. We hope you'll take pleasure in knowing that you're improving and so are your relationships. Finally, when the chance arises, help others do the same. Help friends, loved ones, and coworkers learn to master their own high-stakes discussions. Help strengthen organizations, solidify families, heal communities, and shore up nations one person—one crucial conversation—at a time.

Endnotes

Chapter 1

1. Hermann Simon, *Hidden Champions: Lessons from 500 of the World's Best Unknown Companies* (Boston: Harvard Business School Press, 1996), 195.

2. Clifford Notarius and Howard Markman, *We Can Work It Out: Making Sense of Marital Conflict* (New York: G.P. Putnam's Sons, 1993), 20–22, 37–38.

3. Allen Beck et al., *Survey of State Prison Inmates, 1991* (Washington, DC: U.S. Department of Justice, 1993), 3–5, 6, 11, 13, 16.

4. Dean Ornish, *Love and Survival: The Healing Power of Intimacy* (New York: HarperCollins Publishers, 1998), 63.

5. Ornish, *Love and Survival: The Healing Power of Intimacy*, 54–56.

Chapter 2:

1. Olivia Barker, "4 Studies Aim to Reduce, Resolve Medical Mistakes," *USA Today*, Dec. 8, 1999.

Chapter 6

1. The Arbinger Institute, *Leadership and Self-deception: Getting out of the Box* (San Francisco: Berrett-Koehler, June 2000), 72–74.

Chapter 12

1. Sydnor B. Penick, R. Filion, S. Ross Fox, Albert Stunkard, "Behavior Modification in the treatment of Obesity," *Psychosomatic Medicine* 33 (1971): 49–55.

2. Elliot Aronson, *The Social Animal* (New York: W.H. Freeman & Co., 1984), 25.

3. Yuichi Shoda, Walter Mischel, and Philip K. Peake, "Predicting adolescent cognitive and self-regulatory competencies from preschool delay of gratification," *Developmental Psychology* 26 (1990): 978–86.

Index

About VitalSmarts

An innovator in corporate training and organizational performance, VitalSmarts helps teams and organizations achieve the results they care about most. With award-winning training products based on more than 30 years of ongoing research, VitalSmarts has helped more than 300 of the Fortune 500 realize significant results using a proven method for driving rapid, sustainable and measurable change in behaviors. VitalSmarts has been ranked twice by *Inc.* magazine as one of the fastest-growing companies in America and has taught more than 2 million people worldwide.

VitalSmarts is home to multiple training offerings, including Crucial Conversations®, Crucial Confrontations™, and Influencer™. Each course improves key organizational outcomes by focusing on high-leverage skills and strategies. Along with *Influencer*, their latest book, the VitalSmarts authors have written two *New York Times* bestsellers, *Crucial Conversations* and *Crucial Confrontations*. VitalSmarts also offers on-site consulting, research, executive team development, and speaking engagements.

www.vitalsmarts.com

About the Authors

This award-winning team of authors—now joined by leading researcher David Maxfield—previously produced the two *New York Times* bestsellers, *Crucial Conversations: Tools for Talking when Stakes are High* (2002) and *Crucial Confrontations: Tools for Resolving Broken Promises, Violated Expectations, and Bad Behavior* (2005).

Kerry Patterson has authored award-winning training programs and led multiple long-term change efforts. He received the prestigious 2004 BYU Marriott School of Management Dyer Award for outstanding contribution in organizational behavior. He did doctoral work in organizational behavior at Stanford University.

Joseph Grenny is an acclaimed keynote speaker and consultant who has designed and implemented major corporate change initiatives for the past 20 years. He is also a cofounder of Unitus, a nonprofit organization that helps the world's poor achieve economic self-reliance.

David Maxfield is a leading researcher and frequent conference speaker on topics ranging from dialogue skills to performance improvement. He did doctoral work in psychology at Stanford University, where he studied personality theory and interpersonal-skill development.

Ron McMillan is a sought-after speaker and consultant. He cofounded the Covey Leadership Center, where he served as vice president of research and development. He has worked with leaders ranging from first-level managers to corporate executives on topics such as leadership and team development.

Al Switzler is a renowned consultant and speaker who has directed training and management initiatives with dozens of Fortune 500 companies worldwide. He is on the faculty of the Executive Development Center at the University of Michigan.

Award-winning Training from VitalSmarts

VitalSmarts is home to multiple training offerings, including Crucial Conversations®, Crucial Confrontations™, and the brand new Influencer™ Training.

Based on more than 30 years of ongoing research, VitalSmarts training helps people transform ideas into action and action into results. Each course improves key individual, team, and organizational outcomes by teaching high-leverage skills and strategies.

Crucial Conversations® Training

Drive results by learning to speak with complete candor and complete respect, no matter the issues or the individuals involved. Create alignment, resolve disagreements, surface the best ideas, and make decisions with unity and conviction.

Crucial Confrontations™ Training

Ensure flawless execution with a step-by-step process for improving accountability and addressing performance gaps. Achieve the results you want by learning to motivate without using power and to enable without taking over.

NEW—Influencer™ Training

Diagnose the real reasons behind the problems most organizations face. Use eight powerful principles to create sustainable behavior change and overcome persistent problems.

To receive more information on training from VitalSmarts, mail in the card found in the back of this book, call 1-800-449-5989, or go online to www.vitalsmarts.com.